THE
BIG
BOOK OF
WOK & STIR-FRY

THE
BIG
BOOK OF
WOK & STIR-FRY

Your complete guide to successful
stir-fry cooking

Love Food ® is an imprint of Parragon Books Ltd

Parragon
Queen Street House
4 Queen Street
Bath BA1 1HE, UK

Copyright © Parragon Books Ltd 2009

Love Food ® and the accompanying heart device is a trademark of Parragon Books Ltd

ISBN: 978-1-4075-6443-2

Printed in China

Internal design by Simon Levy
New photography by Charlie Richards
New home economy by Anna Burges-Lumsden, assisted by Mima Sinclair
New recipes, introduction, and cover text by Christine McFadden

Notes for the Reader

This book uses imperial, metric, and US cup measurements. Follow the same units of measurement throughout; do not mix imperial and metric. All spoon measurements are level: teaspoons are assumed to be 5 ml, and tablespoons are assumed to be 15 ml. Unless otherwise stated, milk is assumed to be whole, eggs and individual vegetables such as potatoes are medium, and pepper is freshly ground black pepper.

The times given are an approximate guide only. Preparation times differ according to the techniques used by different people and the cooking times may also vary from those given as a result of the type of oven used. Optional ingredients, variations or serving suggestions have not been included in the calculations.

Recipes using raw or very lightly cooked eggs should be avoided by infants, the elderly, pregnant women, convalescents, and anyone with a chronic condition. Pregnant and breastfeeding women are advised to avoid eating peanuts and peanut products. Sufferers from nut allergies should be aware that some of the ready-prepared ingredients used in the recipes in this book may contain nuts. Always check the packaging before use.

Vegetarians should be aware that some of the ready-prepared ingredients used in the recipes in this book may contain animal products. Always check the packaging before use.

CONTENTS

INTRODUCTION

The workhorse of the Chinese kitchen, the wok has been in use for over 2,000 years. The basic shape remains unchanged, and it is still the essential cooking vessel in the poorest of homes and the most luxurious of restaurants.

Historically, cooking vessels evolved for a number of reasons, a key issue being the type of fuel available. This, in turn, dictated the design and the type of food that could be cooked. In China, fuel was mainly wood, charcoal, or animal dung. Supplies were meager and unpredictable, and much of Chinese cuisine is, therefore, based on poverty, and coping with the harsh conditions commonplace in a predominately agrarian society. The cooking method had to make efficient use of whatever precious fuel was available, and the pan had to heat up quickly. The wok's conical shape and high flaring sides were a masterpiece of design in that respect. Made of metal, it conducted heat quickly, creating a small, but intensely hot area at the bottom. This made it possible for bite-size morsels of food to be quickly stir-fried using relatively little fuel and cooking oil.

The wok was designed for use over the traditional Chinese "pit stove"—a charcoal or wood fire set below a rectangular "fire bench" in which holes or pits were recessed to hold the wok in place. The wok sat snugly in the holes, the wide flaring sides preventing it from dropping into the fire below. The heat rising from the fuel was directed to the bottom of the wok, and no heat escaped around the edges.

Nowadays, pit-style stoves are heated with natural gas, but they follow the same principle with concentrically sloping grates or burners recessed below the stove's surface. The stoves in restaurants and communal kitchens can accommodate gigantic woks for boiling water, and cooking huge quantities of rice or soup. At the other end of the scale, the wok may be used over the simplest of braziers, which were, and still are, the mainstay of the kitchen for poverty-stricken families.

MULTIPURPOSE COOKING VESSEL

Thanks to its unique shape, the wok can cope with virtually all types of food and cooking techniques. Once the bottom is hot, the heat spreads through the entire inside surface, creating a far greater cooking surface than Western pots and pans with vertical sides. This, in turn, creates a range of cooking temperatures in one pan—pieces of food that have been seared in the bottom of the wok can be pushed up the sides to continue cooking at a slower rate. Meanwhile, another ingredient for the same dish is added, and cooked at high heat in the bottom.

Although most often used for stir-frying, the wok can also be used for steaming, boiling, braising, deep-frying, pan-frying, and smoking. The curved cooking surface means that a large amount of

liquid will heat up more quickly, while the wide diameter lets sauces or soups reduce quickly, creating rich complex flavors in the process.

There are two basic wok designs: the Cantonese and the Pau or Peking, both of which are used throughout China. The Cantonese has two rounded handles that make it easier to use when full of liquid—during steaming or deep-frying, for example. The Pau wok has one long handle and is more convenient, and safer too, for stir-frying. The pan is held in one hand and shaken, while the food is turned with a long-handled ladle or spoon held in the other. The long handle distances the cook from the intense heat and hot oil. Some long-handled woks have a small, round handle on the opposite side, which comes in handy when carrying the hot wok from stove to table.

MATERIALS

Woks were traditionally made of cast iron, which maintains a steady, even heat. It is worth noting that Chinese cast-iron woks are thinner and lighter than the Western equivalent. They heat up more quickly and also form a more stable layer of seasoning that prevents food from sticking (see Seasoning a Wok, page 10). The downside is that they are prone to shattering if mishandled or dropped. Western cast-iron woks, on the other hand, are sturdier but slow to heat up and cool down, making all-important temperature control during stir-frying more difficult. They are also heavier, causing undue strain on the wrist during the continual single-handed tossing and stirring needed for a stir-fry.

Currently, the most widely used material is carbon steel. Steel woks are relatively light in weight, conduct heat evenly, and are quick to heat up. However, they vary widely in price and quality. The best are made with two sheets of carbon steel that are formed into shape by hand hammering. You can identify them by the small ridges and dimples on the inside of the wok. The lowest quality are stamped from a single sheet of steel, and likely to distort after a while. They also tend to develop a "hot spot" that causes food to burn and stick.

HEALTH BENEFITS

Thanks to its versatility, the wok can be used for healthy ways of cooking. Stir-frying lets you enjoy the pleasure of fried food without an unhealthy amount of oil. Unlike a standard skillet with a wide, flat bottom, the wok requires little oil to lubricate the food—all that's needed is a tablespoon or so in the bottom. If you're counting calories, you can even use a nonstick cooking spray. Because of the high temperature, the food cooks very quickly without soaking up oil. Once cooked, it is pushed up the sloping sides of the wok and the oil drains back to the bottom.

Steaming is another healthy option, and is easy to do in a wok (see Basic techniques, page 12). It is perfect for vegetables, and tender items, such as fish and chicken. The moist environment means no fat is needed, and fewer nutrients leach into the cooking water because the food does not come in contact with it.

ASIAN CUISINES

Although the wok originated in China, similar cooking vessels are used in East, Southeast, and Southern Asia. Depending on cuisine, they are used in conjunction with other pots and pans, or, as in China's case, they may be the primary cooking vessel.

The shape and name vary depending on country. In Japan, the wok is known as a chukanabe (literally "Chinese pot"). It is shallower and flatter, and used like a regular skillet. The dare-oh of Burma is a rounded, deep pan similar to a wok. It is made of brass or cast iron and has a looped handle on either side. The Indonesian wajan is deeper with straighter sides, while the Vietnamese chao is smaller and shallower. In Malaysia, the wok is called a kuali (small wok) or kawa (big wok). Perhaps the best-known variation is the Indian karahi, a type of flat-bottomed wok with two round handles.

Cuisines may vary from country to country and region to region, but many of the basic cooking styles and techniques have their roots in the use of the wok, even though other cooking vessels may be used as well.

CHINA

As vast as the United States, China spans many degrees of latitude, resulting in radical variations in topography and climate. It is this diversity that lies behind intriguing variations in regional cooking.

In Beijing in the north, the cooking is homely and robust, famous for lamb and duck as well as roast and barbecued dishes. However, the wok is essential for braising hearty stews, deep-frying whole fish, and stir-frying "seaweed" — a typical dish of the region. The wok is also used for cooking noodles, which are the staple rather than rice.

Canton in the south offers an astonishing melting pot of culinary feasts. The region is renowned for top-notch seafood and fresh fruit and vegetables, and it is here that the wok takes center stage. The cooks excel at stir-fries and steamed dim sum (stuffed dumplings), and are eager to experiment with ingredients from abroad.

Located around the Yangtze delta in the east, Shanghai cuisine is a mixture of styles, characterized by rich complex flavors, and the lavish use of the dark soy sauce, for which the delta is renowned. The wok's versatility is ideal for the region's slow-cooked braises, delicate soups, deep-fried fish dishes, and stir-fried rice.

Known as "the land of plenty," Sichuan in the west produces an enormous variety of vegetables, fungi, and fish that are frequently used in rich, heavily sauced dishes cooked in the wok. Sichuan is also famous for smoked duck, a three-stage dish cooked entirely in the wok. The duck is first smoked, then steamed to get rid of excess fat, and finally deep-fried until the meat falls apart.

SOUTHEAST ASIA: INDONESIA, MALAYSIA, AND THAILAND

As in Chinese cuisine, the wok is a vital piece of kitchen equipment. Without the lid, it is perfect for simmering the region's famous green and red curries; the wide surface allows just the right kind of rapid evaporation needed to reduce the sauce. The initial stir-frying of curry spices also takes place in the wok, where the intense heat at the bottom quickly brings out their fragrance. With the lid in place, the wok is used for cooking rice by absorption—a method that requires less water and fuel than boiling.

The wok is particularly important in regions of Southeast Asia where fuel is in short supply: the arid northeast of Thailand, for example, where wood is difficult to find, and the central plains, which have been cleared of forests and converted to rice paddies. In the well-forested north, however, easy access to fuel allows a greater choice of cooking techniques, such as broiling, grilling, and roasting, or lengthy simmering in enormous cauldrons.

INDIA

Like China, India's vast size, and radical variations in topography and climate, result in highly regional cuisines. The diversity is most obvious in the contrast between the rich meat-based dishes of the north, and the vegetarian and fish-based cuisine of the south, where rice is the staple food.

The varied cuisine calls for a variety of cooking vessels. These include conventional saucepans and skillets, as well as the karahi, an Indian version of the Chinese wok. It is used for deep-frying or slowly simmering meat, poultry, seafood, and bean dishes. Many Indian homes have two karahis: a deep one with a narrow top that is used for deep-frying, and a shallower one with a much wider top that is used for occasional stir-frying, pan-frying, and simmering.

ESSENTIAL EQUIPMENT

You don't need a great deal of special equipment to produce authentic Asian-style food, because there is usually an equivalent Western utensil. Useful items are listed below, the most indispensable being a wok and a cleaver.

Wok

The wok's conical shape makes it particularly suitable for stir-frying—the food continually falls to the center where the heat is most intense, so it cooks in a few minutes. Some woks have a slightly flattened bottom for use on a ceramic or electric burner. If fitted with a lid and a stand, a wok can also be used for deep-frying, steaming, and braising.

Woks come in various sizes and materials. Carbon steel conducts heat evenly and quickly, but needs scrupulous drying to prevent rust, and seasoning to prevent sticking. Cast iron is also good, but it is heavy and, like carbon steel, needs drying and seasoning. Anodized aluminum is reasonably maintenance-free, and a good choice for the beginner. Stainless steel looks impressive, but food tends to stick and burn, and it is also harder to keep clean.

For family-sized meals, you will need a roomy wok about 14 inches/35 cm wide. A 10 inch/ 25 cm wok comes in handy for a single serving, or stir-frying a few vegetables.

For stir-frying, use a wok with a long, wooden handle. Wood will stay cool despite the intense heat of the wok. A hollow, metal handle will also remain reasonably cool. Some woks have two round handles instead of a long one. This type may be used for deep-frying, braising, and steaming.

Seasoning a wok:

A new steel or iron wok should be scrubbed to get rid of any rust or factory oil. Place it over medium heat to dry. While still hot, smear all over with a wad of paper towels soaked in cooking oil. Repeat two or three times using clean paper towels. Let cool, then rinse and dry thoroughly.

Cleaning and maintenance:

Wash with hot water but no detergent—it will remove the seasoned coating. Dry over medium heat. Coat with a thin film of oil to prevent rusting.

Cleaver

A cleaver has a rigid, rectangular blade that tapers abruptly to a razor-sharp, beveled edge. It is a multipurpose tool that may be used to slice, dice, fillet, shred, crush, and chop all kinds of food. The back of the blade can be used for pounding, while the flat side comes in handy for transferring ingredients from cutting board to wok.

Cleavers come in different weights, sizes, and materials. The heaviest are for chopping bones, while the lighter ones are for slicing meat and fish, and preparing vegetables. Traditional cleavers are made of carbon steel, which is susceptible to rust and will discolor after contact with acidic foods. They need wiping rather than washing, and should be given a light coating of vegetable oil to prevent rusting.

The best modern cleavers are made of high-carbon, no-stain steel, which is relatively rust-free and has a superior cutting edge.

Cutting board

It's a good idea to have at least two boards: one for raw poultry, meat, and fish, and another for vegetables and herbs. A plastic board is best for poultry, because it can be cleaned in the dishwasher, where the heat will sanitize it.

The traditional Chinese cutting board is a thick slab made with a single cross section of tree trunk. Western boards are made with jointed sections of wood that are prone to splitting and warping. The sturdiest are made with bamboo, or a smooth, tight-grained hardwood, such as maple, beech, or cherry. The board should be about $1^1/2$ inches/4 cm thick to absorb the impact of repeated chopping and to resist warping.

Steamer

The traditional Chinese bamboo steamer has gaps in the bamboo that let excess moisture escape, preventing the food from becoming waterlogged. Bamboo steamers come in a range of sizes, and can be stacked in a wok, or pan of boiling water, so you can cook several dishes at the same time.

Ladle

The Chinese use a special ladle for stir-frying. It has a wide, shallow bowl that is ideal for lifting, tossing, and turning, and an extra-long handle to distance you from the heat. There are also wire mesh ladles for scooping up deep-fried foods.

BASIC TECHNIQUES

Chopping

Cut fresh ingredients into small, even-size pieces, so that they cook in the same amount of time. Slicing meat and vegetables diagonally increases the surface area in contact with the hot oil, and speeds up cooking.

Stir-frying

Before you begin, have all the ingredients measured and prepared. The wok must be very hot before you add any oil—hold your hand flat just above the bottom until you can feel the heat. Using a long-handled ladle, or long, wooden, cooking chopsticks, constantly stir and toss the ingredients, so that they all come in contact with the hot oil and are evenly cooked.

Deep-frying

Use enough oil to form a depth of about 2 inches/5 cm. Heat over a medium–high heat until a faint haze appears. If the oil is not hot enough, the food will become soggy instead of crisp. Cook in small batches—overcrowding lowers the temperature of the oil, and causes uneven cooking. Remove the food with a wire ladle or tongs, and drain thoroughly on paper towels.

Braising

Braising is generally used for tougher cuts of meat, and vegetables with dense flesh. The ingredients are briefly stir-fried, then simmered in stock until tender.

Steaming

This method is used in China to cook whole fish, dumplings, vegetables, and morsels of poultry and meat. The ingredients must be very fresh. Place the food on a heatproof plate, or in a perforated container above boiling liquid in the bottom of a wok. Cover with a lid to trap the steam, which then permeates the food. Depending on size and density, food may be steamed for as little as 10 minutes, or up to 2 or 3 hours.

PANTRY INGREDIENTS

You will need basic seasonings, oils, and various other pantry items, many of which you will probably already have. Most are easily found in supermarkets, health food stores, and Chinese grocers. More obscure items are available by mail order or on-line.

Alcohols for flavoring

Rice wine is widely used in China. It imparts a rich, mellow flavor to marinades, stir-fries, and braised dishes. A good-quality, pale, dry sherry is a reasonable substitute.

Mirin is a Japanese sweet rice wine. It is used in dressings and marinades, and is an essential ingredient in the sticky, brown teriyaki sauce used for glazing broiled or grilled meats.

Baby sweetcorn

Available fresh or canned, the cobs have a sweet flavor and irresistible crunchy texture.

Bamboo shoots

Sold presliced in cans. Once opened, they will keep for up to a week in the refrigerator, covered in fresh water.

Bean sauce

Made from yellow or black fermented soybeans, mixed with flour, salt, and spices.

Black beans

Small, black, fermented soybeans with a distinctive flavor and aroma.

Dried fungi

Valued for texture as well as flavor, Chinese dried fungi include cloud ears, wood ears, "black" mushrooms, and shiitake. Straw mushrooms, grown on rice straw, are bite-size, and available canned or dried.

Dried noodles

Noodles are made with different flours: wheat, rice, mung bean, and buckwheat. They range from thin, round threads to broad, flat ribbons. Cook according to the package directions, because timings vary between brands.

Five-spice powder

A Chinese spice blend that includes star anise, cassia, cloves, fennel seeds, and Sichuan pepper. Use it sparingly in marinades and sauces. It can be stored in an airtight container for at least a year.

Hoisin sauce

A thick, brown, sweet-and-spicy sauce, made from fermented soybean paste, garlic, vinegar, sugar, spices, and other flavorings. Used as a dipping sauce with other ingredients, and as a glaze for roasted meat. It can be kept in the refrigerator for months.

Oils

Peanut oil is best for stir-frying and deep-frying. It has a neutral flavor, and can be heated to a higher temperature than most oils. Canola and sunflower oils are useful vegetable oils.

Toasted sesame oil has a rich, nutty flavor. A few drops are sprinkled over dishes just before serving. It may also be used sparingly, in combination with peanut oil, for stir-frying.

Oyster sauce

A thick, brown, richly flavored sauce, popular in southern China. Made with oysters, soy sauce, salt, and spices. It has a salty, slightly fishy flavor, which dissipates during cooking. It can be kept in the refrigerator for months.

Rice vinegar

Japanese white rice vinegar is amber-colored, with a clean, tart flavor. It is used for flavoring sushi rice. Chinese white rice vinegar is sharper, but also good with rice. Chinese brown rice vinegar is fruitier, and useful for marinades and dressings. Black rice vinegar is mellow and sweet, and used in slow-cooked caramelized duck or pork dishes.

Sichuan pepper

These are tiny, reddish brown husks from the berries of the prickly ash tree. Widely used in hot and spicy dishes of the Sichuan region in China, the husks are numbing rather than hot, and have a strong, lemony flavor.

Soy sauce

A Chinese staple made from fermented soybeans and wheat flour, used both for cooking and at the table. Light soy sauce is more suitable for vegetable, poultry, and seafood dishes, soups, and dipping sauces. Dark soy sauce is slightly thicker and stronger. It is used in "red-cooked" stews, and goes well with beef and lamb.

Shoyu is a Japanese soy sauce that is slightly sweeter and less salty than Chinese light soy sauce. Tamari is a rich, dark Japanese-style sauce, made without wheat.

Sugar

Sugar is used in savory dishes to balance the saltiness of soy and fish sauce, and the sourness of tamarind. Jaggery (also called palm sugar) is used in Southeast Asia. It is sold in compressed brown blocks and has a distinctive caramel flavor.

Tamarind

Made with the pulp extracted from the pods of the tamarind tree. It comes in compressed blocks, which are dissolved in hot water, or as a prepared paste sold in jars. It has a sour, lemony flavor.

Thai fish sauce

A watery, brown, salty liquid made with fermented fish, with a powerful aroma and flavor. Widely used in Southeast Asia, it imparts a special richness to dishes. The fishy flavor dissipates during cooking. Best bought in small bottles—once opened, it should be used within a few weeks.

Tofu (bean curd)

Made with curds from coagulated soybean milk. The curds are molded into creamy white blocks that are compressed until "silken" or "firm." Firm tofu can be sliced into cubes and stir-fried, but needs cooking carefully because it disintegrates if stirred too much. Tofu can be kept for a few days in the refrigerator, if covered with fresh water.

Water chestnuts

Crisp, mildly flavored tubers available peeled and canned. They add pleasing texture to stir-fries, spring rolls, and noodle dishes.

White peppercorns

White peppercorns are preferred in China and Thailand, where specks of black pepper are considered unsightly. Use whole white peppercorns, and grind them as required.

Wrappers

Wonton skins or wrappers are thin, silky squares made from wheat flour, egg, and water. They are stuffed with tasty fillings, and folded into various shapes before deep-frying, steaming, or serving in soup. Spring roll wrappers are larger, paper-thin, and made with rice or wheat flour.

STOCK

Chinese stock is essential for authentic-tasting soups; ordinary stock or stock cubes simply do not have the right flavor. It is also invaluable when a small amount of liquid is required—it will give your dishes an extra special flavor. Stock will keep for 4–5 days in the refrigerator, or can be frozen and defrosted as required.

BASIC CHINESE STOCK

Makes about 6 cups

Ingredients

2 lb/900 g chicken pieces, such as wings, thighs, and drumsticks, coarsely chopped
2 lb/900 g pork spareribs
1 lb/450 g unsmoked ham without rind, in one piece
16 cups water
2³/₄-inch/7-cm thick piece fresh ginger, unpeeled and thickly sliced
1 celery stalk, coarsely chopped
1 carrot, coarsely chopped
3 large scallions, green parts included, halved lengthwise
2 tsp Chinese rice wine or dry sherry

1 Put the chicken, pork, and ham in a large saucepan and just cover with water. Quickly bring to a boil, then drain in a colander and rinse away the foam under cold, running water. Wash out the pan.

2 Return the meat to the pan, and cover with the 16 cups of water. Add the ginger, celery, carrot, and scallions, and slowly bring back to a boil, skimming off any additional foam that forms. Reduce the heat to a very gentle simmer, and cook, uncovered, for 2 hours.

3 Strain the stock through a colander, reserving the liquid and discarding the solids. Pour the liquid through a cheesecloth-lined strainer. Pour back into the pan and add the rice wine. Bring to a boil, then simmer for 2–3 minutes.

4 Pour into containers, let cool, then store in the refrigerator. Once thoroughly chilled, remove the solidified fat from the surface.

SPICY BEEF STOCK

Makes about 6 cups

Ingredients

3 lb 5 oz/1.5 kg beef brisket, or boneless shin of beef, cut into large chunks
12 cups water
1 small onion, quartered
2-inch/5-cm thick piece fresh ginger, unpeeled and thickly sliced
2 inch/5 cm cinnamon stick
5 star anise pods
1 tsp black peppercorns
1 tsp salt

1 Put the beef in a large saucepan with enough water to cover. Quickly bring to a boil, then drain in a colander and rinse away the foam under cold, running water. Wash out the pan.

2 Return the meat to the saucepan with the 12 cups of water, the onion, ginger, cinnamon stick, star anise, black peppercorns, and salt. Slowly bring back to a boil, skimming off any additional foam that forms. Reduce the heat to a very gentle simmer, and cook, uncovered, for 2 hours.

3 Strain the stock through a colander, reserving the liquid and discarding the solids. Pour the liquid through a cheesecloth-lined strainer. Pour into containers, let cool, then store in the refrigerator. Once thoroughly chilled, remove the solidified fat from the surface.

DIPPING SAUCES AND STANDARD SEASONINGS

Traditional dipping sauces and seasonings are served with many Chinese dishes. The spiced salt mixture is a tasty condiment for deep-fried foods.

SCALLION DIPPING SAUCE

Ingredients

4 tbsp finely chopped scallions
4 tbsp finely chopped fresh ginger
2 tbsp light soy sauce
1 tsp rice vinegar
4 tbsp canola oil

Handwritten annotations in left margin: 1 T, 1 T, 1/2 T, 1/4 teas, 1 T

1 Combine the ingredients in a bowl, and whisk very thoroughly until well blended. For a smooth sauce, puree in a blender.

SOY-GINGER DIPPING SAUCE

Ingredients

3 tbsp soy sauce
2 tsp finely chopped fresh ginger

1 Combine the soy sauce and ginger in a small serving bowl. Let stand for 15 minutes to let the flavors develop.

SPICED SALT AND PEPPER

Ingredients

1 tbsp Sichuan pepper
1 tsp white peppercorns
2-inch/5-cm piece cinnamon stick, broken
2 star anise pods
5 tbsp sea salt flakes
1 tsp sugar

1 Dry-fry the Sichuan pepper, white peppercorns, cinnamon, and star anise in a wok over a medium heat, shaking the pan, until the Sichuan pepper begins to smoke and smell fragrant. Grind to a coarse powder with the salt, using an electric coffee grinder or a hefty mortar and pestle. Stir in the sugar, then store in an airtight container for up to 2 months.

APPETIZERS

VIETNAMESE BEEF & NOODLE SOUP

Puree the shallots, garlic, and ginger in a food processor or blender, pulsing several times until the puree is fairly smooth.

Heat a wok over a medium–high heat, then add the oil. Stir-fry the paste for 2 minutes, being careful to avoid letting it burn. Add the beef and stir-fry for 1 minute until brown, then pour in 4 cups of the stock. Bring to a rapid boil, skimming off any scum that forms. Add the crushed peppercorns, then reduce the heat and gently simmer for 30–35 minutes, or until the meat is tender.

Meanwhile, prepare the noodles according to the package directions.

When the meat is tender, stir in any sticky residue that has formed at the edge of the wok. Add the remaining stock, the lime juice, fish sauce, salt, and sugar. Simmer for a few minutes.

Drain the noodles and divide between individual soup bowls. Ladle the meat and broth over the top. Serve with the garnishes sprinkled over the soup.

SERVES 4

4 shallots, chopped

1 large garlic clove, chopped

2 tsp finely chopped fresh ginger

1 tbsp peanut oil

1 lb/450 g sirloin steak, external fat removed, cut into ½-inch/1-cm cubes

5¼ cups Spicy Beef Stock (see page 16)

1 tsp white peppercorns, crushed

5½ oz/150 g flat rice noodles

juice of 1 lime

2 tsp Thai fish sauce

½ tsp salt

½ tsp sugar

to garnish

4 scallions, shredded

slivers of fresh red chile

3 tbsp torn cilantro leaves

3 tbsp torn basil leaves

lime wedges

SPICY BEEF & MUSHROOM WONTONS

To make the filling, combine the ground steak, scallion, mushrooms, garlic, and ginger in a bowl. Mix the soy sauce, salt, pepper, five-spice seasoning, and cornstarch to a thin paste. Add the paste to the beef mixture, then stir in half the beaten egg (use the remainder in another recipe). Stir with a fork until well mixed.

Separate the wonton squares and place on a tray, rotating them so one corner is facing toward you. Cover with a clean damp dish towel to prevent cracking. Working with one square at a time, place a slightly rounded teaspoon of filling in the bottom corner, ½ inch/1 cm away from the point. Fold the point over the filling, then roll up two thirds of the wrapper, leaving a point at the top. Moisten the right- and left-hand corners with a dab of water. Fold one corner over the other and press lightly to seal into a bishop's miter shape. Continue until all the wontons are filled.

Heat a large wok over a high heat. Pour in the oil and heat to 180°C/350°F, or until a cube of bread browns in 30 seconds. Deep-fry the wontons in batches for 4–5 minutes, until golden brown. Remove with tongs and drain on crumpled paper towels. Serve with the dipping sauce.

MAKES 12–15

filling

4 oz/125 g ground, lean sirloin or top round steak

1 scallion, green part included, finely chopped

2 button mushrooms, finely chopped

1 small garlic clove, finely chopped

½ tsp finely chopped fresh ginger

½ tsp soy sauce

¼ tsp salt

¼ tsp white pepper

⅛ tsp Chinese five-spice seasoning

½ tsp cornstarch

1 egg, beaten

12–15 square wonton wrappers

peanut oil, for deep-frying

Soy-Ginger Dipping Sauce (see page 17), to serve

HOT & SOUR PORK SOUP WITH BAMBOO SHOOTS

SERVES 4

2 large shiitake mushrooms

5 cups Basic Chinese Stock
   (see page 16)

4½ oz/125 g pork tenderloin,
   thinly sliced into narrow shreds

1 oz/25 g canned sliced bamboo
   shoots, drained

3½ oz/100 g firm tofu, cut into
   ½-inch/1-cm cubes

1 tbsp Chinese rice wine or dry
   sherry

2 tsp light soy sauce

1 tbsp rice vinegar

¼ tsp white pepper, or more to
   taste

2 scallions, some green parts
   included, thinly sliced
   diagonally, to garnish

few drops sesame oil, to garnish

Remove the hard stalks from the mushrooms and slice the caps thinly. Cut the slices in half.

Bring the stock to a rapid boil in a large wok. Reduce the heat, add the mushrooms, and simmer for 5 minutes. Add the pork, bamboo shoots, and tofu and simmer for another 5 minutes. Add the rice wine, soy sauce, vinegar, and white pepper and simmer for 1 minute.

Ladle into soup bowls and sprinkle with the scallions and a few drops of sesame oil.

SWEET & SOUR SPARERIBS

Combine the marinade ingredients in a bowl with the spareribs and let marinate for at least 20 minutes.

Heat enough oil for deep-frying in a large wok to 350°F/180°C, or until a cube of bread browns in 30 seconds. Deep-fry the spareribs for 8 minutes. Drain and set aside.

To make the sauce, mix together the vinegar, sugar, soy sauce, and ketchup. Set aside.

Heat a wok over a medium–high heat, then add 1 tablespoon of the oil. Stir-fry the bell pepper, onion, and carrot for 2 minutes. Remove and set aside.

Quickly wipe out the wok and reheat. Add the remaining oil and stir-fry the garlic and ginger until fragrant. Add the sauce, then bring back to a boil and add the pineapple chunks. Finally, add the spareribs and the bell pepper mixture. Stir until warmed through and serve immediately.

SERVES 4

1 lb/450 g spareribs, cut into bite-size pieces

1½ tbsp vegetable or peanut oil, plus extra for deep-frying

1 green bell pepper, seeded and cut into 1-inch/2.5-cm chunks

1 small onion, coarsely chopped

1 small carrot, finely sliced

½ tsp finely chopped garlic

½ tsp finely chopped fresh ginger

3½ oz/100 g canned pineapple chunks

marinade
2 tsp light soy sauce

½ tsp salt

pinch of white pepper

sauce
3 tbsp white rice vinegar

2 tbsp sugar

1 tbsp light soy sauce

1 tbsp ketchup

CRISPY PORK DUMPLINGS

To make the filling, put the pork in a bowl and beat in the cilantro, garlic, chile, 1 tablespoon of the cornstarch, the egg white, and salt. Beat together to a thick, smooth texture. With damp hands, shape into 16 equal portions and roll into balls.

Put a pork ball in the center of each wonton wrapper. Make a paste by mixing the remaining cornstarch with the water. Brush the edges of the wrappers with the cornstarch paste and gather them up around the filling to make half into small, sacklike parcels, and the rest into triangular shapes.

Arrange the dumplings in a single layer (in batches if need be) in the top of a steamer and cook over boiling water for 10–15 minutes, until the meat is cooked through.

Heat a large wok over a high heat. Pour in the oil and heat to 350°F/180°C, or until a cube of bread browns in 30 seconds. Deep-fry the parcels for 2–3 minutes, until golden brown and crisp. Drain on paper towels.

Serve hot with chili sauce.

MAKES 16

filling

12 oz/350 g ground pork

2 tbsp finely chopped, fresh cilantro

1 garlic clove, crushed

1 fresh green chile, seeded and chopped

3 tbsp cornstarch

1 egg white

½ tsp salt

16 wonton wrappers

1 tbsp water

vegetable or peanut oil, for deep-frying

chili sauce, to serve

PORK & SHRIMP EGG ROLLS

MAKES 20–25

filling

6 dried Chinese mushrooms, soaked in warm water for 20 minutes

1 tbsp vegetable or peanut oil, plus extra for deep-frying

8 oz/225 g ground pork

1 tsp dark soy sauce

8 oz/225 g fresh or canned bamboo shoots, rinsed and julienned (if using fresh shoots, boil in water first for 30 minutes)

pinch of salt

3½ oz/100 g shrimp, peeled, deveined, and chopped

6 oz/175 g fresh bean sprouts, coarsely chopped

1 tbsp finely chopped scallion

25 egg roll wrappers

1 egg white, lightly beaten

chili sauce, to serve

Squeeze out any excess water from the mushrooms and finely slice, discarding any tough stems.

To make the filling, heat a wok over a medium–high heat, then add the oil. Stir-fry the pork until it changes color. Add the soy sauce, bamboo shoots, mushrooms, and salt. Stir over a high heat for 3 minutes.

Add the shrimp and cook for 2 minutes, then add the bean sprouts and cook for an additional minute. Remove from the heat and stir in the scallion. Let cool.

Place a tablespoon of the filling toward the bottom of a wrapper. Roll once to secure the filling, then fold in the sides to create a 4-inch/10-cm long egg roll and continue to roll up. Seal with egg white.

Heat a large wok over a high heat. Pour in the oil and heat to 350°F/180°C, or until a cube of bread browns in 30 seconds. Cook the egg rolls, in batches, for about 5 minutes, until golden brown and crispy. Serve immediately with the chili sauce.

FRIED LAMB BALLS WITH SCALLION SAUCE

Combine the lamb, garlic, and ginger in a bowl. Mix the soy sauce, wine, salt, sugar, pepper, and cornstarch to a thin paste. Add the paste to the lamb mixture, then stir in the beaten egg. Stir with a fork until well mixed. Pinch off small pieces of the mixture and roll between your palms to form balls the size of a large marble.

Heat a wok over a high heat, add the oil, and when it is almost smoking, add the balls. Fry the balls in batches for 3 minutes, turning half-way through. Drain on crumpled paper towels.

Arrange a bed of shredded Chinese lettuce on a serving platter. Arrange the lamb balls on top and sprinkle with garlic chives. Divide the dipping sauce between two small bowls and serve with the lamb.

⑧

MAKES 36

½ lb — 1 lb/450 g ground lamb

¼ — 1 garlic clove, finely chopped

¼ teas — 1 tsp finely chopped fresh ginger

½ T — 1½ tbsp soy sauce

¼ teas — 1 tsp Chinese rice wine or
dry sherry *MIRIN*

⅛ teas — ½ tsp salt

⅛ teas — ½ tsp sugar

⅛ teas — ½ tsp white pepper

⅛ teas — ½ tbsp cornstarch

¼ — 1 egg, beaten

peanut oil, for frying

snipped garlic chives, to garnish

to serve
shredded Chinese lettuce

Scallion Dipping Sauce
(see page 17)

CHICKEN
NOODLE SOUP

Cook the noodles according to the package directions.

Meanwhile, heat a wok over a medium–high heat, then add the oil. Add the chicken and stir-fry for 5 minutes, or until lightly browned. Add the white part of the scallions, the garlic, and ginger and stir-fry for 2 minutes.

Add the stock, coconut milk, curry paste, peanut butter, and soy sauce. Season to taste with salt and pepper. Bring to a boil, stirring constantly, then simmer for 8 minutes, stirring occasionally. Add the bell pepper, peas, and green scallion tops and cook for an additional 2 minutes.

Drain the noodles, then add them to the wok and heat through. Spoon into serving bowls and serve immediately.

SERVES 4–6

9 oz/250 g medium egg noodles

1 tbsp corn oil

4 skinless, boneless chicken thighs, diced

1 bunch of scallions, sliced

2 garlic cloves, chopped

3/4-inch/2-cm piece fresh ginger, finely chopped

3¾ cups chicken stock

¾ cup coconut milk

3 tsp Thai red curry paste

3 tbsp peanut butter

2 tbsp light soy sauce

1 small red bell pepper, seeded and chopped

½ cup frozen peas

salt and pepper

ASIAN-STYLE GLAZED CHICKEN WINGS

SERVES 4

8 chicken wings, each wing chopped into 3 pieces

5 tbsp peanut oil

6 tbsp Basic Chinese Stock (see page 16) or water

2 tbsp chopped fresh cilantro

marinade

1½ tbsp Chinese rice wine or dry sherry

1 tbsp soy sauce

1 tbsp rice vinegar

1½ tbsp sugar

¾ tsp salt

⅛ tsp Chinese five-spice seasoning

3 tbsp hoisin sauce

1 tsp finely chopped fresh ginger

To make the marinade, combine the wine, soy sauce, and vinegar in a small bowl. Add the sugar, salt, and five-spice seasoning and stir until dissolved. Mix in the hoisin sauce and ginger.

Put the chopped chicken wings in a shallow dish and pour in the marinade, turning the wings to coat. Let stand to marinate for 1 hour at room temperature, or overnight in the refrigerator.

Heat a wok over a high heat, add the oil, and when it is almost smoking, add the chicken wings and marinade. Stir-fry for 5 minutes, then sprinkle with 4 tablespoons of the stock and stir-fry for another 4 minutes.

Using tongs, transfer the wings to a serving dish and sprinkle with the cilantro. Pour off and discard most of the oil from the wok and return to the heat. Add the remaining 2 tablespoons of stock and stir with a wooden spoon until blended, scraping up the sticky sediment. Pour into a small bowl and serve with the wings as a dipping sauce.

KARA-AGE CHICKEN

Cut the chicken into large cubes and put in a bowl. Add the soy sauce, mirin, ginger, and garlic and turn the chicken to coat well. Cover with plastic wrap and let marinate in a cool place for 20 minutes.

Heat a large wok over a high heat. Pour in the oil and heat to 350°F/180°C, or until a cube of bread browns in 30 seconds.

Meanwhile, mix the potato starch with the salt in a bowl. Lift the chicken out of the marinade and shake off any excess. Drop it into the potato starch and coat well, then shake off any excess.

Add the chicken to the oil, in batches, and cook for 6 minutes, or until crisp and brown. Remove, drain on paper towels, and keep hot while you cook the remaining chicken.

Serve with lemon wedges.

SERVES 4

6 skinless, boneless chicken thighs, about 3½ oz/100 g each

4 tbsp shoyu (Japanese soy sauce)

4 tbsp mirin

2 tsp finely grated fresh ginger

2 garlic cloves, crushed

oil, for deep-frying

½ cup potato starch or cornstarch

pinch of salt

lemon wedges, to serve

SHREDDED DUCK WITH CUCUMBER

Stack the cucumber slices, cut into thin strips, and set aside. Combine the sauce ingredients in a small bowl, stirring to dissolve the sugar.

Heat a wok over a medium–high heat, then add the oils. Fry the duck breast pieces for 4–5 minutes, starting skin-side down and turning occasionally, until both the skin and meat are crisp. Transfer with tongs to a cutting board and let cool slightly.

Lower the heat to medium. Stir-fry the shallot and ginger in the remaining oil for about 2 minutes, until golden brown. Remove with a slotted spoon and drain on paper towels.

Remove the crisp skin from the duck pieces and slice into shreds. Remove and discard any excess fat from the meat. Slice the meat into 1/4-inch/5-mm-wide pieces.

Wipe out the wok with paper towels and place over a medium–high heat. Add the duck meat, sauce, and scallions and stir-fry for 2 minutes, until caramelized. Season with salt and pepper, then remove from the heat.

Divide the duck mixture between the lettuce leaves, top with the cucumber strips, shallot, ginger, and crushed peanuts. Roll up into parcels and serve.

SERVES 4

5-cm/2-inch piece cucumber, peeled and thinly sliced

1 tbsp peanut oil

1 tbsp sesame oil

2 duck breasts, weighing 12 oz/350 g in total, cut into large pieces

1 large shallot, halved and sliced into crescents

3/4-inch/2-cm piece fresh ginger, thinly sliced and cut into shreds

2 scallions, shredded

4 large iceberg lettuce leaves, stalks removed

3 tbsp crushed, dry roasted peanuts

salt and pepper

sauce

2 tsp soy sauce

4 tsp oyster sauce

2 tsp Chinese rice wine or dry sherry

3/4 tsp sugar

THAI-STYLE SEAFOOD SOUP

SERVES 4

5 cups fish stock

1 lemongrass stalk, split lengthwise

pared rind of ½ lime or 1 fresh kaffir lime leaf

1-inch/2.5-cm piece fresh ginger, sliced

¼ tsp chili paste, or to taste

4–6 scallions

7 oz/200 g large or medium shrimp, shelled

9 oz/250 g scallops (16–20)

2 tbsp cilantro leaves

salt

finely chopped red bell pepper or fresh red chile rings, to garnish

Heat a large wok over a high heat. Add the stock with the lemongrass, lime rind, ginger, and chili paste. Bring just to a boil, then reduce the heat and simmer, covered, for 10–15 minutes.

Cut the scallions in half lengthwise, then slice crosswise thinly. Cut the shrimp almost in half lengthwise, then thinly slice crosswise. Devein if necessary.

Pour the stock through a strainer, then return to the wok and bring to a simmer. Add the scallions and cook for 2–3 minutes. Taste and season with salt, if needed. Stir in a little more chili paste if you like.

Add the scallops and shrimp and poach for 1 minute, or until they turn opaque and the shrimp curl.

Drop in the cilantro leaves, then ladle the soup into warmed serving bowls, dividing the shellfish evenly, and garnish with bell pepper.

SPICY THAI SOUP WITH SHRIMP

Heat a large wok over a high heat. Add the tamarind paste, chiles, garlic, galangal, fish sauce, sugar, lime leaves, and stock. Bring to a boil, stirring constantly.

Reduce the heat and add the carrots, sweet potato, and baby corn to the mixture in the wok.

Let the soup simmer for 10 minutes, or until the vegetables are just tender.

Stir the cilantro, cherry tomatoes, and shrimp into the soup and heat through for 5 minutes.

Transfer the soup to serving bowls and serve hot.

SERVES 4

2 tbsp tamarind paste

4 fresh red Thai chiles, finely chopped

2 garlic cloves, crushed

1-inch/2.5-cm piece fresh galangal, finely chopped

4 tbsp Thai fish sauce

2 tbsp jaggery or light brown sugar

8 fresh kaffir lime leaves, coarsely torn

4 cups fish stock

1 cup thinly sliced carrots

2 cups diced sweet potato

3½ oz/100 g baby corn, halved

3 tbsp cilantro, coarsely chopped

3½ oz/100 g cherry tomatoes, halved

8 oz/225 g cooked fantail shrimp

SALMON & SHRIMP SPRING ROLLS

Heat a large wok over a high heat, add the salmon, and stir-fry for 1 minute. Remove from the wok with a slotted spoon and put onto a plate. Using the cooking juices from the salmon, stir-fry the vegetables with the five-spice powder until just tender, drain in a colander, then stir in the cooked salmon and shrimp—the mixture should be dry to prevent the rolls from becoming soggy.

Divide the salmon-and-vegetable mixture into 8 portions. Spoon a portion along one short edge of each spring roll wrapper and roll up, tucking in the sides.

Lay the spring rolls on a nonstick baking sheet and spray lightly with vegetable oil, sprinkle with sesame seeds, and bake in a preheated oven for 12–15 minutes, or until golden brown. Serve the spring rolls with plum sauce.

MAKES 8

filling

4½ oz/125 g salmon fillet, skinned, boned, and cut into ⅛-inch/3-mm cubes

2¼ oz/60 g fresh bean sprouts

⅔ cup finely shredded Chinese cabbage

¼ cup finely chopped scallion

½ medium red bell pepper, seeded and finely sliced

¼ tsp five-spice powder

2¼ oz/60 g cooked, shelled shrimp

4 spring roll wrappers, halved widthwise

vegetable oil spray

¼ tsp sesame seeds

plum sauce, to serve

SHRIMP TOAST

MAKES 16

3½ oz/100 g shrimp, shelled and deveined

2 egg whites

2 tbsp cornstarch

½ tsp sugar

pinch of salt

2 tbsp finely chopped cilantro

2 slices day-old white bread

vegetable or peanut oil, for deep-frying

Pound the shrimp to a pulp with a mortar and pestle or with the bottom of a cleaver.

Mix the shrimp with one of the egg whites and 1 tablespoon of the cornstarch. Add the sugar and salt and stir in the cilantro. Mix the remaining egg white with the remaining cornstarch.

Remove the crusts from the bread and cut each slice into 8 triangles. Brush the top of each piece with the egg white-and-cornstarch mixture, then add 1 teaspoon of the shrimp mixture. Smooth the top.

Heat a large wok over a high heat. Pour in the oil and heat to 350°F/180°C, or until a cube of bread browns in 30 seconds. Without overcrowding the wok, cook the toast, shrimp-side up, for about 2 minutes. Turn and cook for an additional 2 minutes, or until beginning to turn golden brown. Drain and serve warm.

CRISP SESAME SHRIMP

Combine the flour and sesame seeds in a bowl. Stir the curry paste, fish sauce, and water together in a pitcher until mixed. Gradually pour the liquid into the flour, stirring constantly, to make a thick batter.

Heat a large wok over a high heat. Pour in the oil and heat to 350°F/180°C, or until a cube of bread browns in 30 seconds. Holding the shrimp by their tails, dip them into the batter, one at a time, then carefully drop into the hot oil. Cook for 2–3 minutes, until crisp and brown. Drain on paper towels.

Serve immediately with chili sauce.

MAKES 20

generous ¾ cup self-rising flour

3 tbsp sesame seeds, toasted or dry-fried

1 tsp Thai red curry paste

1 tbsp Thai fish sauce

⅔ cup water

vegetable or peanut oil, for deep-frying

20 large shrimp, shelled, with tails intact

chili sauce, for dipping

CRISPY CRAB WONTONS

To make the filling, mix the crabmeat, water chestnuts, chile, scallion, cornstarch, sherry, soy sauce, and lime juice together in a bowl.

Spread the wonton wrappers out on a counter and spoon an equal portion of the filling into the center of each wonton wrapper.

Dampen the edges of the wonton wrappers with a little water and fold them in half to form triangles. Fold the 2 bottom corners in toward the center, moisten with a little water to secure, then pinch together to seal.

Heat a large wok over a high heat. Pour in the oil and heat to 350°F/180°C, or until a cube of bread browns in 30 seconds. Deep-fry the wontons in batches for 2–3 minutes, until golden brown and crisp. Remove with a slotted spoon and drain on paper towels.

Serve the wontons hot, garnished with chives and lime slices.

MAKES 24

filling

6 oz/175 g white crabmeat, drained if canned and thawed if frozen, flaked

1¾ oz/50 g canned water chestnuts, drained, rinsed, and chopped

1 small fresh red chile, chopped

1 scallion, chopped

1 tbsp cornstarch

1 tsp dry sherry

1 tsp light soy sauce

½ tsp lime juice

24 square wonton wrappers

vegetable oil, for deep-frying

fresh chives and lime slices, to garnish

CHINESE VEGETABLE SOUP

SERVES 4–6

4 oz/115 g napa cabbage

2 tbsp peanut oil

8 oz/225 g firm tofu, cut into
  ½-inch/1-cm cubes

2 garlic cloves, thinly sliced

4 scallions, thinly sliced
  diagonally

1 carrot, thinly sliced

4 cups vegetable stock

1 tbsp Chinese rice wine

2 tbsp light soy sauce

1 tsp sugar

salt and pepper

Shred the napa cabbage and set aside. Heat a large wok over a high heat, then add the oil. Add the tofu cubes and stir-fry for 4–5 minutes, until browned. Remove from the wok with a slotted spoon and drain on paper towels.

Add the garlic, scallions, and carrot to the wok and stir-fry for 2 minutes. Pour in the stock, rice wine, and soy sauce, then add the sugar and shredded napa cabbage. Cook over a medium heat, stirring, for an additional 1–2 minutes, until heated through.

Season with salt and pepper and return the tofu to the wok. Ladle the soup into bowls and serve.

MUSHROOM & GINGER SOUP

Soak the dried Chinese mushrooms for at least 30 minutes in 1¼ cups of the hot stock. Drain the mushrooms and reserve the stock. Remove the stems of the mushrooms and discard. Slice the caps and reserve.

Cook the noodles according to the package directions. Drain well, rinse under cold water, and drain again. Set aside.

Heat a large wok over a high heat, then add the oil. Add the garlic and ginger, stir, and add the mushrooms. Stir over a high heat for 2 minutes.

Add the remaining stock with the reserved mushroom soaking liquid and bring to a boil. Add the soy sauce. Stir in the bean sprouts and cook until tender.

Divide the noodles among 4 serving bowls and ladle the soup on top. Garnish with cilantro leaves and serve immediately.

SERVES 4

½ oz/15 g dried Chinese mushrooms or 4½ oz/ 125 g portobello or cremini mushrooms

4 cups hot vegetable stock

4½ oz/125 g thin egg noodles

2 tsp corn oil

3 garlic cloves, crushed

1-inch/2.5-cm piece fresh ginger, finely shredded

1 tsp light soy sauce

1 lb/450 g fresh bean sprouts

fresh cilantro leaves, to garnish

CRISPY "SEAWEED"

Remove and discard the tough stalks from the cabbage leaves. Wash the leaves, drain thoroughly, and spread out on paper towels to dry.

Stack a few leaves and roll up tightly. Using a sharp knife, slice crosswise into the thinnest possible shreds. Repeat with the remaining leaves. Spread out the shreds on paper towels and let stand until completely dry.

Heat a large wok over a high heat. Pour in the oil and heat to 180ºC/350ºF, or until a cube of bread browns in 30 seconds. Remove the wok from the heat and add half the shredded leaves. Return the wok to the heat and deep-fry until the shreds begin to float to the surface and become crisp. Remove with a slotted spoon and drain on paper towels. Keep warm while you deep-fry the rest.

Tip the shreds into a warm serving bowl. Combine the sugar and salt and sprinkle over the "seaweed," tossing to mix.

Quickly fry the slivered almonds in the hot oil. Remove with a slotted spoon and sprinkle over the "seaweed." Serve warm or at room temperature.

SERVES 4

9 oz/250 g dark green cabbage leaves

peanut oil, for deep-frying

1 tsp superfine sugar

½ tsp salt

4 tbsp slivered almonds, to garnish

VEGETARIAN SPRING ROLLS

MAKES 20

filling

6 dried Chinese mushrooms, soaked in warm water for 20 minutes

2 oz/55 g cellophane noodles, soaked in warm water for 20 minutes

2 tbsp vegetable or peanut oil

1 tbsp finely chopped fresh ginger

2 medium carrots, julienned

1 cup finely shredded cabbage

1 tbsp finely sliced scallions

1 tbsp light soy sauce

3 oz/85 g soft tofu, cut into small cubes

½ tsp salt

pinch of white pepper

pinch of sugar

20 spring roll skins

1 egg white, lightly beaten

vegetable or peanut oil, for deep-frying

soy sauce, for dipping

To make the filling, squeeze out any excess water from the mushrooms and finely chop, discarding any tough stems. Drain the cellophane noodles and coarsely chop.

Heat a wok over a medium–high heat, then add the oil. Toss in the ginger and cook until fragrant. Add the mushrooms and stir for about 2 minutes. Add the carrot, cabbage, and scallions and stir-fry for 1 minute. Add the cellophane noodles and light soy sauce and stir-fry for 1 minute. Add the tofu and cook for an additional 1 minute. Season with the salt, pepper, and sugar and mix well. Continue cooking for 1–2 minutes, or until the carrot is soft. Remove from the heat and let the mixture cool.

To assemble each roll, place a tablespoon of the filling toward the bottom of a skin. Roll once to secure the filling, then fold in the sides to create a 4-inch/10-cm roll and continue to roll up. Seal with egg white.

Heat a large wok over a high heat. Pour in the oil and heat to 350°F/180°C, or until a cube of bread browns in 30 seconds. Without overcrowding the pan, cook the rolls in batches for about 5 minutes, or until golden brown and crispy. Serve with a good soy sauce for dipping.

WONTONS

To make the filling, heat a wok over a high heat, then add the oil. Stir-fry the scallions, mushrooms, and green beans for 1–2 minutes, until softened. Add the corn, stir well to mix, and then push the vegetables to the side. Pour in the egg. Stir until lightly set before incorporating the vegetables and adding the soy sauce, sugar, and salt. Remove the wok from the heat.

Place the wonton wrappers in a pile on a counter. Put a teaspoonful of the filling in the center of the top wrapper. Brush the edges with beaten egg and fold in half diagonally to make a small triangular parcel. Repeat with the remaining wrappers and filling.

Heat a large wok over a high heat. Pour in the oil and heat to 350°F/180°C, or until a cube of bread browns in 30 seconds. Add the parcels, in batches, and deep-fry for 3–4 minutes, until golden brown. Remove from the wok with a slotted spoon and drain on paper towels. Keep warm while you cook the remaining wontons. Serve hot with plum or chili sauce.

MAKES 24

filling
2 tbsp vegetable or peanut oil

6 scallions, chopped

generous 2 cups chopped mushrooms

⅓ cup chopped green beans

¼ cup corn kernels, drained if canned

1 egg, beaten

3 tbsp Thai soy sauce

1 tbsp jaggery or light brown sugar

½ tsp salt

24 wonton wrappers

1 egg, beaten

vegetable or peanut oil, for deep-frying

plum or chili sauce, to serve

PICKLED BABY CUCUMBERS

Heat a wok over a high heat, then add the oil. Cook the cucumbers for 3–5 minutes, until they are bright green. Drain and set aside. When cool, score the skin many times on all sides. Place in a large dish.

Combine the vinegar, salt, sugar, and chiles and pour over the cucumbers, immersing them in the liquid. Let marinate for 24 hours, then serve cold in chunks.

SERVES 4

1 tbsp vegetable or peanut oil, for frying

14 oz/400 g baby cucumbers

2¼ cups white rice vinegar

1 tbsp salt

3 tbsp sugar

3 red Thai chiles, seeded and finely chopped

VEGETABLES & SALADS

CLASSIC STIR-FRIED VEGETABLES

Heat a wok over a high heat, then add 2 tablespoons of the oil.
Stir-fry two thirds of the scallions with the garlic and ginger for
30 seconds.

Add the broccoli, bell pepper, and red cabbage and stir-fry for
1–2 minutes. Mix in the baby corn and mushrooms and stir-fry for
an additional 1–2 minutes.

Finally, add the bean sprouts and water chestnuts and cook for
an additional 2 minutes. Pour in the soy sauce and stir well.

Transfer to warmed dishes and serve immediately, garnished
with the remaining scallions.

SERVES 4

3 tbsp sesame oil

8 scallions, chopped

1 garlic clove, crushed

1 tbsp grated fresh ginger

1 head broccoli, cut into florets

1 yellow or orange bell pepper,
seeded and coarsely chopped

1 cup shredded red cabbage

4½ oz/125 g baby corn

2 cups thinly sliced portobello
mushrooms

5 oz/140 g fresh bean sprouts

9 oz/250 g canned water
chestnuts, drained

4 tsp light soy sauce

SWEET & SOUR VEGETABLES WITH CASHEW NUTS

Heat a wok over a high heat, then add both of the oils. Add the onions and stir-fry for 1–2 minutes, until they begin to soften.

Add the carrots, zucchini, and broccoli and stir-fry for 2–3 minutes. Add the mushrooms, bok choy, sugar, soy sauce, and vinegar and stir-fry for 1–2 minutes.

Meanwhile, heat a dry, heavy-bottom skillet over a high heat, add the cashew nuts, and cook, shaking the skillet frequently, until lightly toasted. Sprinkle the cashew nuts over the stir-fry and serve immediately.

SERVES 4

1 tbsp vegetable or peanut oil

1 tsp chili oil

2 onions, sliced

2 carrots, thinly sliced

2 zucchini, thinly sliced

1 small head broccoli, cut into florets

2 cups sliced white mushrooms

1 small bok choy, halved

2 tbsp jaggery or brown sugar

2 tbsp Thai soy sauce

1 tbsp rice vinegar

scant ½ cup cashew nuts

MIXED VEGETABLES WITH BASIL

SERVES 4

2 tbsp vegetable or peanut oil, plus extra for shallow-frying

2 garlic cloves, chopped

1 onion, sliced

4 oz/115 g baby corn, cut in half diagonally

½ cucumber, peeled, halved, seeded, and sliced

8 oz/225 g canned water chestnuts, drained and rinsed

2 oz/55 g snow peas

2 cups shiitake mushrooms, halved

1 red bell pepper, seeded and thinly sliced

1 tbsp light brown sugar

2 tbsp light soy sauce

1 tbsp Thai fish sauce

1 tbsp rice vinegar

8–12 sprigs fresh Thai basil

cooked plain rice, to serve

Heat a wok over a high heat, then add the oil. Stir-fry the garlic and onion for 1–2 minutes. Add the baby corn, cucumber, water chestnuts, snow peas, mushrooms, and bell pepper and stir-fry for 2–3 minutes, until they begin to soften.

Add the sugar, soy sauce, fish sauce, and vinegar and gradually bring to a boil. Let simmer for 1–2 minutes.

Meanwhile, heat a wok over a high heat and add enough oil for shallow-frying. When hot, add the basil sprigs and cook for 20–30 seconds, until crisp. Remove with a slotted spoon and drain on paper towels.

Garnish the vegetable stir-fry with the crispy basil and serve immediately with cooked rice.

BAMBOO SHOOTS WITH TOFU

Squeeze out any excess water from the mushrooms and finely slice, discarding any tough stems. Blanch the bok choy in a large pan of boiling water for 30 seconds. Drain and set aside.

Heat a large wok over a high heat. Pour in the oil and heat to 350°F/180°C, or until a cube of bread browns in 30 seconds. Cook the tofu cubes until golden brown. Remove, then drain and set aside.

Heat a wok over a high heat, then add 1 tablespoon of the oil. Toss in the mushrooms and bok choy and stir. Add the tofu and bamboo shoots with the oyster and soy sauces. Heat through and serve.

SERVES 4–6

3 dried Chinese mushrooms, soaked in warm water for 20 minutes

2 oz/55 g baby bok choy

1 lb/450 g firm tofu, cut into 1-inch/2.5-cm squares

1 tbsp vegetable or peanut oil, plus extra for deep-frying

4 oz/115 g fresh or canned bamboo shoots, rinsed and finely sliced (if using fresh shoots, boil in water first for 30 minutes)

1 tsp oyster sauce

1 tsp light soy sauce

STIR-FRIED
BEAN SPROUTS

Heat the wok over a medium–high heat, then add the oil. Stir-fry the bean sprouts with the scallion for about 1 minute. Add the salt and sugar and stir.

Serve immediately.

SERVES 4

1 tbsp vegetable or peanut oil

8 oz/225 g fresh bean sprouts

2 tbsp finely chopped scallion

½ tsp salt

pinch of sugar

SPICY GREEN BEANS

SERVES 4

8 oz/225 g green beans, cut
   diagonally into 3–4 pieces

2 tbsp vegetable or peanut oil

4 dried chiles, cut into 2–3 pieces

½ tsp Sichuan peppers

1 garlic clove, finely sliced

6 thin slices fresh ginger

2 scallions, white part only,
   cut diagonally into thin pieces

pinch of sea salt

Blanch the beans in a large pan of boiling water for 30 seconds. Drain and set aside.

Heat a wok over a medium–high heat, then add 1 tablespoon of the oil. Stir-fry the beans for about 5 minutes, or until they begin to wrinkle. Remove from the wok and set aside.

Add the remaining oil to the wok and stir-fry the chiles and peppers until they are fragrant. Add the garlic, ginger, and scallions and stir-fry until they begin to soften. Add the beans and toss to mix, then add the sea salt and serve immediately.

STIR-FRIED BROCCOLI

Heat a wok over a medium–high heat, then add the oil. Stir-fry the broccoli for 4–5 minutes.

In a small bowl, combine the soy sauce, cornstarch, sugar, ginger, garlic, and chile flakes. Add the mixture to the broccoli. Cook over a gentle heat, stirring constantly, for 2–3 minutes, until the sauce thickens slightly.

Transfer to a serving dish, garnish with the sesame seeds, and serve immediately.

SERVES 4

2 tbsp vegetable oil

2 medium heads broccoli, cut into florets

2 tbsp light soy sauce

1 tsp cornstarch

1 tbsp superfine sugar

1 tsp grated fresh ginger

1 garlic clove, crushed

pinch of hot chile flakes

1 tsp toasted sesame seeds, to garnish

CAULIFLOWER & BEANS WITH CASHEW NUTS

Heat the wok over a medium–high heat, then add both of the oils. Stir-fry the onion and garlic until softened. Add the curry paste and stir-fry for 1–2 minutes.

Add the cauliflower and beans and stir-fry for 3–4 minutes, until softened. Pour in the stock and soy sauce and let simmer for 1–2 minutes. Serve immediately, garnished with the cashew nuts.

SERVES 4

1 tbsp vegetable or peanut oil

1 tbsp chili oil

1 onion, chopped

2 garlic cloves, chopped

2 tbsp Thai red curry paste

1 small cauliflower, cut into florets

6 oz/175 g yard-long beans, cut into 3-inch/7.5-cm lengths

$^2/_3$ cup vegetable stock

2 tbsp Thai soy sauce

scant 1 cup toasted cashew nuts, to garnish

CHUNKY POTATOES WITH CILANTRO LEAVES

SERVES 6–8

4 potatoes, peeled and cut into large chunks

1 tbsp vegetable or peanut oil, plus extra for frying

3½ oz/100 g pork, not too lean, finely chopped or ground

1 green bell pepper, seeded and finely chopped

1 tbsp finely chopped scallions, white part only

2 tsp salt

½ tsp white pepper

pinch of sugar

2–3 tbsp cooking water reserved from the potatoes

2 tbsp chopped cilantro leaves

Boil the potatoes in a large pan of boiling water for 15–25 minutes, or until cooked. Drain, reserving some of the water.

Heat a wok over a medium–high heat, then add plenty of oil. Cook the potatoes until golden. Drain and set aside.

Heat a clean wok over a medium–high heat, add 1 tablespoon of the oil, and stir-fry the pork, bell pepper, and scallions for 1 minute. Season with the salt, pepper, and sugar and stir-fry for an additional 1 minute.

Stir in the potato chunks and add the water. Cook for 2–3 minutes, or until the potatoes are warmed through. Turn off the heat, then stir in the cilantro and serve warm.

SICHUAN FRIED EGGPLANT

Heat a wok over a medium–high heat, then add 2 tablespoons of the oil. Cook the eggplant pieces for 3–4 minutes, or until lightly browned. Drain on paper towels and set aside.

Heat a clean wok over a medium–high heat, then add the remaining oil. Add the chili bean sauce and stir-fry rapidly, then add the ginger and garlic and stir until fragrant. Add the stock, sugar, and light soy sauce. Toss in the fried eggplant pieces and let simmer for 2 minutes. Stir in the scallions and serve.

SERVES 4

4 tbsp vegetable or peanut oil, for frying

4 eggplants, halved lengthwise and cut diagonally into 2-inch/5-cm pieces

1 tbsp chili bean sauce

2 tsp finely chopped fresh ginger

2 tsp finely chopped garlic

2–3 tbsp chicken stock

1 tsp sugar

1 tsp light soy sauce

3 scallions, finely chopped

STIR-FRIED BUTTERNUT SQUASH

Slice the squash crosswise at the point where the rounded part meets the neck. Remove the skin from each piece. Quarter the rounded part, and remove the seeds and fibers. Slice lengthwise into thin segments. Slice the neck in half lengthwise, then crosswise into thin semicircles.

Remove and discard the tough stalks from the mushrooms and thinly slice the caps.

Heat a wok over a medium–high heat, then add the oil. Add half the crushed peppercorns and coriander seeds. Stir for a few seconds, then add the squash in small batches. Fry for 5–7 minutes, carefully turning with tongs, until lightly browned and just tender. Sprinkle with sea salt flakes. Using a slotted spoon, transfer to a large strainer set over a bowl.

Add the mushrooms to the wok and fry for 4–5 minutes, using some of the oil drained from the squash. Add the garlic and lemon zest and fry for another minute. Sprinkle with sea salt flakes and the rest of the coriander seeds and peppercorns. Add to the squash.

Pour any oil drained from the vegetables into the wok. Stir in the vinegar and stock and simmer for a few seconds, until slightly reduced.

Arrange the spinach on individual serving plates. Pile the vegetables on top, then pour over the juices from the wok. Sprinkle with cilantro and serve at once with rice.

SERVES 2

1 butternut squash, weighing about 18 oz/500 g

6 large shiitake mushrooms

5 tbsp canola oil

½ tsp white peppercorns, crushed

½ tsp coriander seeds, crushed

sea salt flakes

2 large garlic cloves, thinly sliced

finely grated zest of ½ lemon

½ tbsp rice vinegar

4 tbsp chicken or vegetable stock

2 good handfuls of baby spinach, stalks removed

chopped fresh cilantro leaves, to garnish

cooked plain rice, to serve

STIR-FRIED TOFU WITH BEAN SPROUTS

SERVES 2–3

1½ tbsp light soy sauce

1 tbsp oyster sauce

2 tbsp chicken stock or Basic
Chinese Stock (see page 16)

peanut oil, for deep-frying

12 oz/350 g firm tofu, cubed

2 large garlic cloves, thinly sliced

4 oz/115 g snow peas, halved
diagonally

4 scallions, sliced diagonally into
1-inch/2.5-cm pieces

5 oz/140 g fresh bean sprouts

salt and pepper

½ bunch garlic chives, or
ordinary chives, snipped
into 1-inch/2.5-cm lengths

few drops sesame oil

Combine the soy sauce, oyster sauce, and chicken stock in a
small bowl and set aside.

Heat a wok over a high heat, then add the oil to a depth of
about ¾ inch/2 cm. When the oil is almost smoking, add the tofu
and fry for 5–7 minutes, until golden brown, turning with tongs.
Remove with a slotted spoon and drain on paper towels. Season
with salt and black pepper.

Pour the oil from the wok, reserving 1 tablespoon (use the rest
in another dish), and wipe out the wok. Heat the reserved oil,
add the garlic, and stir-fry for a few seconds to flavor the oil. Add
the snow peas and scallions and stir-fry for 2 minutes.

Add the bean sprouts and soy sauce mixture. Stir-fry for
1 minute, then add the fried tofu and stir to mix. Sprinkle
with the chives and a few drops of sesame oil and
serve at once.

SICHUAN NUMBING BEEF SALAD

Slice the beef into ½ x 1½ inches/1 x 4 cm pieces. Combine the marinade ingredients and pour over the beef. Marinate at room temperature for 30 minutes, or in the refrigerator for up to 2 days.

Cook the noodles according to the package directions and let cool. Snip into shorter lengths. Whisk the dressing ingredients until well blended. Combine the noodles, onion, radishes, and peppery leaves in a large bowl. Whisk the dressing again and pour two thirds of it over the salad. Toss to distribute the noodles, then divide between individual serving plates.

Heat a wok over a medium–high heat, then add the peanut oil and Sichuan pepper. Stir for a few seconds to flavor the oil. Add the beef and marinade and stir-fry for 4–5 minutes, until caramelized. Remove with a slotted spoon and scatter over the salad. Pour over the remaining dressing.

SERVES 4

12 oz/350 g porterhouse steak, external fat removed

3½ oz/90 g egg noodles

1 small red onion, halved and thinly sliced

6 radishes, sliced

4 good handfuls of peppery leaves, such as tatsoi, mustard greens, and arugula

1½ tbsp peanut oil

1 tsp Sichuan pepper, crushed

marinade

4 tsp Chinese rice wine or dry sherry

½ tbsp soy sauce

4 tsp sugar

2 tbsp hoisin sauce

1-inch/2.5-cm piece fresh ginger, squeezed in a garlic press

dressing

2 tsp Sichuan pepper, crushed

1½ tbsp light soy sauce

1½ tbsp rice vinegar

2 tbsp cold-pressed sesame oil

PORK & CUCUMBER SALAD

Trim the pork of any sinew and fat, and thinly slice diagonally. Cut each slice in half lengthwise. Put in a bowl with the scallions.

Peel the cucumber, halve lengthwise, and scoop out the seeds. Thinly slice diagonally and put in a bowl.

Next make the marinade. Using a large mortar and pestle, pound the chopped chiles and the sugar to a watery, red paste. Add the Thai fish sauce, lime juice, and rice vinegar, stirring to dissolve the sugar. Pour into a pitcher. Pour one half over the pork and onions and one half over the cucumber. Marinate for 1 hour, then drain the cucumber and reserve its marinade.

Put the shredded lettuce, cilantro, and mint in a bowl and toss to mix. Divide between individual serving plates. Arrange the cucumber slices on top and dress with the reserved marinade.

Mix the nuts with the lime zest, salt, and sugar.

Drain the pork and discard the marinade. Toss with the kechap manis. Heat a wok over a high heat, then add the oils. Stir-fry the pork for 5 minutes, until cooked through and slightly caramelized. Arrange the pork slices on top of the cucumber and sprinkle with the nut mixture. Serve at once.

SERVES 4

1 lb/450 g pork tenderloin

6 scallions, halved lengthwise and sliced into 3

1 cucumber

4 handfuls shredded Iceberg lettuce

1 cup cilantro leaves

½ cup mint leaves

4 tbsp lightly crushed dry-roast peanuts

finely grated zest of 1 lime

1 tsp salt

1 tsp sugar

1 tbsp kechap manis, or dark soy sauce

1 tbsp peanut oil

2 tsp sesame oil

marinade

2 small fresh red chiles, seeded and finely chopped

4 tbsp sugar

3 tbsp Thai fish sauce

4 tbsp lime juice

4 tbsp rice vinegar

CHINESE CHICKEN SALAD

SERVES 4

3 boneless, skinless chicken breasts, weighing 1 lb/450 g in total, cut into bite-size pieces

2 tsp soy sauce

¼ tsp white pepper

2 tbsp peanut oil, plus extra for deep-frying

1¾ oz/50 g thin rice noodles

½ head Chinese cabbage, thinly sliced diagonally

3 scallions, green parts included, sliced diagonally

¼ cup almonds with skin, sliced lengthwise

2 tsp sesame seeds, to garnish

dressing

5 tbsp olive oil

3 tbsp rice vinegar

3 tbsp light soy sauce

a few drops sesame oil

salt and pepper

Sprinkle the chicken with the soy sauce and white pepper. Combine the dressing ingredients and whisk to blend.

Heat a wok over a high heat, then add the 2 tablespoons of peanut oil. Stir-fry the chicken for 4–5 minutes, until brown and crisp. Drain on paper towels and let cool. Wipe out the wok.

Pour enough peanut oil for deep-frying into the wok. Heat until almost smoking, then fry a few noodles at a time, until puffed up and crisp. Drain on paper towels.

Arrange the Chinese cabbage in a shallow serving dish. Place the noodles in a pile on top of the leaves, on one side of the dish. Arrange the chicken, scallions, and almonds in the remaining space. Whisk the dressing again and pour over the salad. Dress with the sesame seeds and serve.

GINGERED CHICKEN & VEGETABLE SALAD

Cut the chicken into large cubes, each about 1 inch/2.5 cm. Mix the scallions, ginger, garlic, and 2 tablespoons of oil together in a shallow dish and add the chicken. Cover and let marinate for at least 3 hours. Lift the meat out of the marinade and set aside.

Heat the wok over a medium–high heat, then add the remaining oil. Cook the onion for 1–2 minutes, then add the rest of the vegetables except the cucumber. Cook for 2–3 minutes, until just tender. Add the cucumber, half the soy sauce, the sugar, and the basil and mix gently.

Prepare the noodles according to the package directions and drain well. Sprinkle the remaining soy sauce over them and arrange on plates. Top with the cooked vegetables.

Add a little more oil to the wok, if necessary, and cook the chicken over a high heat until browned on all sides. Arrange the chicken cubes on top of the salad and serve hot or warm.

SERVES 4

4 skinless, boneless chicken breasts

4 scallions, chopped

1-inch/2.5-cm piece ginger, chopped finely

4 garlic cloves, crushed

3 tbsp vegetable or peanut oil, plus extra for frying, if needed

1 onion, sliced

2 garlic cloves, chopped

4 oz/115 g baby corn, halved

4 oz/115 g snow peas, halved lengthwise

1 red bell pepper, seeded and sliced

3-inch/7.5-cm piece cucumber, peeled, seeded, and sliced

4 tbsp Thai soy sauce

1 tbsp jaggery or light brown sugar

few Thai basil leaves

6 oz/175 g fine egg noodles

RICE & TURKEY SALAD

Set aside 3 tablespoons of the chicken stock and bring the remainder to a boil in a large pan. Add the rice and cook for 30 minutes, or until tender. Drain and let cool slightly.

Meanwhile, heat a wok over a high heat, then add 1 tablespoon of the oil. Stir-fry the turkey over a medium heat for 3–4 minutes, or until cooked through. Using a slotted spoon, transfer the turkey to a dish. Add the snow peas and mushrooms to the wok and stir-fry for 1 minute. Add the reserved stock, bring to a boil, then reduce the heat, cover, and let simmer for 3–4 minutes. Transfer the vegetables to the dish and let cool slightly.

Thoroughly mix the rice, turkey, snow peas, mushrooms, nuts, cilantro, and garlic chives together, then season to taste with salt and pepper. Drizzle with the remaining corn oil and the vinegar and garnish with fresh garlic chives. Serve warm.

SERVES 4

4 cups chicken stock

scant 1 cup mixed long-grain and wild rice

2 tbsp corn oil

8 oz/225 g skinless, boneless turkey breast, trimmed of all visible fat and cut into thin pieces

5 oz/140 g snow peas

4 oz/115 g oyster mushrooms, torn into pieces

¼ cup shelled pistachio nuts, finely chopped

2 tbsp chopped fresh cilantro

1 tbsp snipped fresh garlic chives

salt and pepper

1 tbsp balsamic vinegar

fresh garlic chives, to garnish

DUCK SALAD

SERVES 4

4 boneless duck breasts,
   skin on

1 lemongrass stalk, broken into
   three and each cut in half
   lengthwise

3 tbsp vegetable or peanut oil

2 tbsp sesame oil

1 tsp Thai fish sauce

1 fresh green chile, seeded and
   chopped

2 tbsp red curry paste

½ fresh pineapple, peeled and
   sliced

3-inch/7.5-cm piece cucumber,
   peeled, seeded, and sliced

3 tomatoes, cut into wedges

1 onion, thinly sliced

dressing

juice of 1 lemon

2 garlic cloves, crushed

1 tsp jaggery or light brown sugar

2 tbsp vegetable or peanut oil

Unwrap the duck and let the skin dry out overnight in
the refrigerator.

The following day, slash the skin side 5–6 times. Mix the
lemongrass, 2 tablespoons of the vegetable oil, all the sesame
oil, fish sauce, chile, and curry paste together in a shallow dish
and place the duck breasts in the mixture. Turn to coat and rub
the marinade into the meat. Let chill for 2–3 hours.

Heat a wok over a medium-high heat, then add the remaining
oil. Cook the duck, skin-side down over a medium heat, for
3–4 minutes, until the skin is browned and crisp and the meat is
cooked most of the way through.

Turn the breasts over and cook until browned and the meat is
cooked to your liking.

Meanwhile, arrange the pineapple, cucumber, tomatoes, and
onion on a platter. Mix the dressing ingredients together and
pour over the top.

Lift the duck out of the wok and slice thickly. Arrange the duck
slices on top of the salad and serve immediately.

CHINESE SHRIMP SALAD

Prepare the noodles according to the package directions. Drain thoroughly and pat dry with paper towels.

Heat a wok over a high heat, then add the sunflower oil. Add the noodles and stir-fry for 5 minutes, tossing frequently.

Remove the wok from the heat and add the sesame oil, sesame seeds, and bean sprouts, tossing to mix well.

Mix the mango, scallions, radishes, shrimp, soy sauce, and sherry together in a separate bowl. Toss the shrimp mixture with the noodles. Alternatively, arrange the noodles around the edge of a serving plate and pile the shrimp mixture into the center. Serve at once.

VEGETABLES & SALADS

104

SERVES 4

9 oz/250 g thin egg noodles

3 tbsp sunflower oil

1 tbsp sesame oil

1 tbsp sesame seeds

4 oz/115 g fresh bean sprouts

1 mango, peeled, pitted, and sliced

6 scallions, sliced

2¾ oz/75 g radishes, sliced

12 oz/350 g cooked, shelled shrimp

2 tbsp light soy sauce

1 tbsp sherry

CARAMELIZED TUNA SALAD

To make the dressing, heat a small wok over a high heat. Add the oil and fry the ginger and chile for a few seconds. Add the soy sauce, Thai fish sauce, and tamarind paste. Stir for 30 seconds, then add the sugar and stir until dissolved. Remove the wok from the heat and set aside.

Rinse the bean sprouts in boiling water and drain. Blot dry with paper towels. Peel the cucumber, halve lengthwise, and scoop out the seeds. Thinly slice the flesh diagonally.

Put the bean sprouts, cucumber, cilantro, and mint leaves in a bowl. Season with a pinch of salt and a few drops of sesame oil. Toss to combine, then divide between individual serving plates.

Heat a large wok over a high heat, then add the sesame and peanut oils. Quickly stir-fry the tuna, turning with tongs, until colored on the outside but still slightly red in the middle. Arrange the tuna chunks on top of the salad.

Reheat the dressing, thinning with a spoonful of water if necessary, and pour over the tuna. Sprinkle with the crushed peanuts and serve at once.

SERVES 4

7 oz/200 g fresh bean sprouts

4-inch/10-cm piece of cucumber

1½ cups cilantro leaves

1½ cups mint leaves

1 tsp sesame oil, plus a few drops for drizzling

1 tbsp peanut oil

1 lb/450 g fresh tuna, cut into 1-inch/2.5-cm chunks

salt

2 tbsp salted roasted peanuts, crushed, to garnish

dressing

2 tsp canola oil

1 tsp finely chopped fresh ginger

½–1 small fresh red chile, seeded and finely chopped

4 tbsp light soy sauce

1 tbsp Thai fish sauce

1 tbsp tamarind paste

⅓ cup soft brown sugar

RAINBOW
SALAD

SERVES 3–4

6 large shiitake mushrooms

1 red bell pepper

10 scallions, green parts included

6 carrots

3 tbsp canola oil

8 baby corn, halved diagonally

10 oz/275 g fresh bean sprouts

salt

a few small mint leaves, to garnish

4 tbsp toasted coconut ribbons,
    to garnish

dressing

½–1 green chile, seeded and finely
    chopped

1 tsp sugar

1½ tbsp lime juice

2 tsp Thai fish sauce

2 tbsp chopped mint

2 tbsp canola oil

6 tbsp coconut cream

salt

First make the dressing. Using a mortar and pestle, pound the chile and sugar to a watery, green paste. Add the lime juice, Thai fish sauce, and a pinch of salt and stir to dissolve the sugar. Pour into a blender with the mint, oil, and coconut cream. Puree until smooth and set aside.

Remove and discard the tough stalks from the mushrooms and thinly slice the caps. Halve, core, and seed the bell pepper and slice into thin slivers. Halve the scallions lengthwise, then slice into 1-inch/2.5-cm lengths, keeping the green and white parts separate.

Using a swivel peeler, shave the carrots into thin slivers.

Heat a wok over a high heat, then add the 3 tablespoons of canola oil. Stir-fry the mushrooms, bell pepper, baby corn, and the white parts of the scallions for 2 minutes. Add the carrots, bean sprouts, green parts of the scallions, and salt to taste. Toss for 1 minute, until the vegetables are only just cooked and still crunchy.

Transfer to a colander set over a bowl and let cool. Discard any drained liquid and tip the vegetables into a serving bowl. Toss with the dressing, then sprinkle with mint leaves and the toasted coconut ribbons. Serve at room temperature.

EGGPLANT &
ONION SALAD

Heat a wok over a high heat, then add half of the oil. Cook the onions together for 1–2 minutes, until just softened but not browned. Lift out and set aside.

Add the eggplant cubes, in batches if necessary, adding more oil as needed, until they are crisp and golden brown.

Return the onions to the wok and add the curry paste, soy sauce, and sugar. Add the creamed coconut and water and cook until dissolved. Stir in most of the cilantro, the basil, and the parsley.

Toss the arugula in the chili sauce and serve with the eggplant and onion salad. Garnish with the remaining herbs.

SERVES 4

4 tbsp vegetable or peanut oil

1 onion, sliced

4 shallots, chopped finely

4 scallions, sliced

12 oz/350 g eggplants, cubed

2 tbsp Thai green curry paste

2 tbsp Thai soy sauce

1 tsp jaggery or light brown sugar

4 oz/115 g creamed coconut, chopped

3 tbsp water

small handful of fresh cilantro, chopped

few Thai basil leaves, chopped

small handful of fresh parsley, chopped

2½ cups arugula leaves

2 tbsp sweet chili sauce

HOT & SOUR VEGETABLE SALAD

Heat a wok over a high heat, then add the oils. Sauté the onion and ginger for 1–2 minutes, until they begin to soften. Add the vegetables and stir-fry for 2–3 minutes, until they have softened slightly. Remove from the heat and set aside.

Mix the dressing ingredients together. Transfer the vegetables to a serving plate and drizzle the dressing over. Serve warm or let the flavors develop and serve cold.

SERVES 4

2 tbsp vegetable or peanut oil

1 tbsp chili oil

1 onion, sliced

1-inch/2.5-cm piece ginger, grated

1 small head broccoli,
    cut into florets

2 carrots, cut into short thin sticks

1 red bell pepper, seeded and cut
    into squares

1 yellow bell pepper, seeded and
    cut into thin pieces

2 oz/55 g snow peas, halved

2 oz/55 g baby corn, halved

dressing

2 tbsp vegetable or peanut oil

1 tsp chili oil

1 tbsp rice wine vinegar

juice of 1 lime

½ tsp Thai fish sauce

MEAT

BEEF CHOW MEIN

Combine all the marinade ingredients in a bowl and marinate the beef for at least 20 minutes.

Cook the noodles according to the package directions. Drain, then rinse under cold water and set aside.

Heat a wok over a medium–high heat, then add the oil. Stir-fry the beef for about 1 minute, or until it has changed color. Stir in the onion and cook for 1 minute, then add the bell pepper and bean sprouts. Cook until any water from the vegetables has evaporated.

Add the salt, sugar, rice wine, and soy sauces. Stir in the noodles and toss for 1 minute. Finally, stir in the scallion and serve.

SERVES 4

10 oz/280 g beef tenderloin, cut into slivers

8 oz/225 g egg noodles

2 tbsp vegetable or peanut oil

1 onion, finely sliced

1 green bell pepper, finely sliced

4 oz/115 g fresh bean sprouts

1 tsp salt

pinch of sugar

2 tsp Chinese rice wine

2 tbsp light soy sauce

1 tbsp dark soy sauce

1 tbsp finely shredded scallion

marinade

1 tsp light soy sauce

dash of sesame oil

½ tsp Chinese rice wine

pinch of white pepper

STIR-FRIED BEEF WITH BEAN SPROUTS

Slice the scallions lengthwise into thin strips, reserving some for a garnish.

Heat a wok over a medium–high heat, then add the oil. Add the scallions, garlic, and ginger and stir-fry for 2–3 minutes, until softened. Add the beef and continue stir-frying for 4–5 minutes, or until evenly browned.

Add the bell pepper and stir-fry for an additional 3–4 minutes. Add the chile and bean sprouts and stir-fry for 2 minutes. Mix the lemongrass, peanut butter, coconut milk, rice vinegar, soy sauce, and sugar together in a bowl, then stir into the wok.

Meanwhile, cook the egg noodles according to the package directions. Drain and stir into the wok, tossing to mix evenly. Season to taste with salt and pepper. Sprinkle with the reserved scallions and serve hot.

SERVES 4

1 bunch of scallions

2 tbsp corn oil

1 garlic clove, crushed

1 tsp finely chopped fresh ginger

1 lb 2 oz/500 g lean beef tenderloin, cut into thin strips

1 large red bell pepper, seeded and sliced

1 small fresh red chile, seeded and chopped

12 oz/350 g fresh bean sprouts

1 small lemongrass stalk, finely chopped

2 tbsp smooth peanut butter

4 tbsp coconut milk

1 tbsp rice vinegar or white wine vinegar

1 tbsp soy sauce

1 tsp light brown sugar

9 oz/250 g medium egg noodles

salt and pepper

HOT SESAME
BEEF

SERVES 4

1 lb 2 oz/500 g beef tenderloin,
   cut into thin strips

1½ tbsp sesame seeds

½ cup beef stock

2 tbsp light soy sauce

2 tbsp grated fresh ginger

2 garlic cloves, chopped finely

1 tsp cornstarch

½ tsp chile flakes

3 tbsp sesame oil

1 large head broccoli,
   cut into florets

1 orange bell pepper, seeded and
   thinly sliced

1 fresh red chile, seeded and
   thinly sliced

1 tbsp chili oil, to taste

1 tbsp chopped fresh cilantro,
   to garnish

Mix the beef with 1 tablespoon of the sesame seeds in a small
bowl. In a separate bowl, whisk together the stock, soy sauce,
ginger, garlic, cornstarch, and chile flakes.

Heat a wok over a medium–high heat, then add 1 tablespoon
of the sesame oil. Stir-fry the beef for 2–3 minutes. Remove and
set aside.

Discard any oil left in the wok, then wipe with paper towels to
remove any stray sesame seeds. Heat the remaining oil in the
wok, add the broccoli, orange bell pepper, chile, and chili oil, and
stir-fry for 2–3 minutes. Stir in the stock mixture, cover, and let
simmer for 2 minutes.

Return the beef to the wok and let simmer until the juices
thicken, stirring occasionally. Cook for another 1–2 minutes.

Sprinkle with the remaining sesame seeds. Serve garnished
with chopped cilantro.

DAN DAN
NOODLES

Heat a wok over a medium–high heat, then add the oil. Toss in the chile and Sichuan pepper, then add the meat and stir rapidly. When the meat has changed color, add the light soy sauce and continue to cook until the meat is well browned. Carefully mix the sauce ingredients together and pour into 4 serving dishes.

Cook the noodles according to the package directions. When cooked, drain and divide among the dishes.

Top with the meat mixture, then sprinkle with the roasted peanuts and serve at once. Mix well before eating.

SERVES 4

1 tbsp vegetable or peanut oil

1 large dried chile, seeded and snipped into 3 pieces

½ tsp Sichuan pepper

3½ oz/100 g ground beef

2 tsp light soy sauce

10½ oz/300 g fine rice noodles

1 tbsp chopped roasted peanuts

sauce

1 tbsp preserved vegetables

½ tsp lightly roasted and crushed Sichuan pepper

scant ½ cup chicken stock

1 tsp black rice vinegar

1 tsp chili oil

1 tsp dark soy sauce

1 tbsp light soy sauce

1 tbsp sesame paste

a few drops of sesame oil

2 scallions, finely chopped

BEEF NOODLES WITH OYSTER SAUCE

To make the marinade, stir the ingredients together in a nonmetallic bowl. Stir in the beef so all the slices are coated, then set aside to marinate for at least 15 minutes.

Meanwhile, cook the noodles according to the package instructions. Drain, rinse, and drain again, then set aside.

Heat a wok over a medium–high heat, then add 1 tablespoon of the oil. Add the asparagus and stir-fry for 1 minute. Tip the beef and marinade into the wok, standing back because it will splutter, and continue stir-frying until the beef is cooked to your taste, about 1½ minutes for medium. Remove the beef and asparagus from the wok and set aside.

Heat the remaining oil in the wok and stir-fry the garlic, ginger, and onion for about 1 minute, until the onion is soft. Add the stock, rice wine, and oyster sauce and bring to a boil, stirring. Return the beef and asparagus to the wok, along with the noodles. Use 2 forks to mix all the ingredients together and stir around until the noodles are hot. Sprinkle with the sesame seeds.

SERVES 4

10½ oz/300 g sirloin steak, thinly sliced

9 oz/250 g thick egg noodles

2 tbsp peanut or corn oil

8 oz/225 g fresh asparagus spears, woody ends cut off and chopped

2 large garlic cloves, finely chopped

½-inch/1-cm piece fresh ginger, finely chopped

½ red onion, thinly sliced

4 tbsp beef or vegetable stock

1½ tbsp rice wine

2–3 tbsp oyster sauce

toasted sesame seeds, to garnish

marinade

1 tbsp light soy sauce

1 tsp sesame oil

2 tsp rice wine

GINGER BEEF WITH YELLOW BELL PEPPERS

SERVES 4

1 lb 2 oz/500 g beef tenderloin,
  cut into 1-inch/2.5-cm cubes

2 tsp peanut oil

2 garlic cloves, crushed

2 tbsp grated fresh ginger

pinch of chile flakes

2 yellow bell peppers, seeded and
  thinly sliced

4½ oz/125 g baby corn

6 oz/175 g snow peas

cooked noodles drizzled with
  sesame oil, to serve

marinade

2 tbsp soy sauce

2 tsp peanut oil

1½ tsp superfine sugar

1 tsp cornstarch

To make the marinade, mix the soy sauce, oil, sugar, and cornstarch in a bowl. Stir in the beef, then cover with plastic wrap and set aside to marinate for 30 minutes.

Heat a wok over a medium–high heat, then add the oil. Add the garlic, ginger, and chile flakes and cook for 30 seconds. Stir in the yellow bell peppers and baby corn and stir-fry for 2 minutes. Add the snow peas and cook for another minute.

Remove the vegetables from the wok. Add the beef and marinade to the wok and stir-fry for 3–4 minutes, or until cooked to taste. Return the vegetables to the wok, mix well, and cook until all the ingredients are heated through. Remove from the heat and serve with the cooked noodles.

MARINATED BEEF WITH VEGETABLES

To make the marinade, mix the sherry, soy sauce, cornstarch, sugar, garlic, and oil in a bowl. Add the beef to the mixture and cover with plastic wrap. Set aside to marinate for 30 minutes, then remove the beef and discard the marinade.

Heat a wok over a medium–high heat, then add 1 tablespoon of the oil. Stir-fry the beef for 2 minutes, until medium–rare. Remove from the wok and set aside.

Combine the cornstarch and soy sauce in a bowl and set aside. Heat the remaining 2 tablespoons of oil in the wok, add the broccoli, carrots, and snow peas and stir-fry for 2 minutes.

Add the stock, cover the wok, and cook for one minute. Stir in the spinach, beef, and the cornstarch mixture. Cook until the juices boil and thicken. Serve with cooked rice or noodles.

SERVES 4

1 lb 2 oz/500 g sirloin steak, cut into thin strips

3 tbsp sesame oil

½ tbsp cornstarch

½ tbsp soy sauce

1 head broccoli, cut into florets

2 carrots, cut into thin strips

4 oz/125 g snow peas

½ cup beef stock

9 oz/250 g baby spinach, shredded

cooked plain rice or noodles, to serve

marinade

1 tbsp dry sherry

½ tbsp soy sauce

½ tbsp cornstarch

½ tsp superfine sugar

2 garlic cloves, finely chopped

1 tbsp sesame oil

BEEF WITH BLACK PEPPER & LIME

Pound the steak with the blunt side of a knife. Slice diagonally across the grain into thin bite-size pieces, and put in a shallow bowl.

Combine the sugar, pepper, soy sauce, chile, garlic, and half the lime juice in a bowl, mixing well. Pour over the beef, stirring to coat. Marinate at room temperature for 1 hour, or overnight in the refrigerator.

Arrange the Chinese cabbage in a shallow serving dish. Scatter with the red onion slices.

Heat a wok over a high heat, then add the oil. Stir-fry the beef for 3 minutes. Add the Thai fish sauce and the remaining lime juice, and stir-fry for an additional 1 minute.

Tip the meat and juices over the Chinese cabbage and onion, then scatter over the mint. Garnish with the lime wedges, and serve immediately with cooked rice.

SERVES 2–3

12 oz/350 g flank steak

½ tbsp jaggery or light brown sugar

1 tbsp black peppercorns, crushed

4 tsp soy sauce

1 red Thai chile, seeded and finely chopped

½ head garlic, cloves crushed

2 tbsp lime juice

½ head Chinese cabbage, sliced

½ red onion, thinly sliced

1½ tbsp peanut oil

½ tsp Thai fish sauce

3 tbsp chopped fresh mint

lime wedges, to garnish

cooked plain rice, to serve

BEEF & BOK CHOY STIR-FRY

SERVES 2–3

12 oz/350 g flank steak

2 tbsp peanut oil

1 shallot, chopped

2 tsp finely chopped fresh ginger

1 fresh red chile, seeded and
thinly sliced

12 oz/350 g bok choy, stalks sliced
into 1-inch/2.5-cm squares,
leaves into wide ribbons

1 tbsp cornstarch

2 tbsp beef stock or water

3 tbsp chopped fresh cilantro

marinade

2 tbsp soy sauce

1½ tbsp Chinese rice wine or dry
sherry

½ tsp sugar

½ tsp black pepper

¼ tsp salt

Pound the steak with the blunt side of a knife. Slice diagonally
across the grain into thin bite-size pieces and put in a
shallow bowl.

Combine the marinade ingredients in a bowl and pour over the
beef, stirring to coat. Marinate at room temperature for 1 hour,
or overnight in the refrigerator.

Heat a wok over a medium–high heat, then add the oil. Stir-fry
the shallot, ginger, and chile for 1 minute. Increase the heat to
high and add the beef and marinade. Stir-fry for 3 minutes. Add
the bok choy stalks and stir-fry for 1 minute. Add the leaves and
stir-fry for an additional minute.

Mix the cornstarch and stock to a smooth paste. Add to the
wok and stir-fry for 1 minute, until slightly thickened. Transfer
to a warmed serving dish and sprinkle with the cilantro. Serve
immediately.

BEEF WITH MIXED MUSHROOMS

Using a mortar and pestle, grind the Sichuan pepper with the salt. Sprinkle over both sides of the meat, pressing in well. Slice the meat diagonally across the grain into thin, bite-size pieces and set aside.

Rinse the mushrooms and dry with paper towels. If using clumping mushrooms, such as enoki and buna shimeji, slice off the root and separate the clump. Slice cremini mushrooms in half.

Mix the cornstarch to a paste with 2 tablespoons of the stock. Add the rice wine and soy sauce, mixing well.

Heat a wok over a medium–high heat, then add 1 tablespoon of the oil. Fry the shallot and ginger for 1 minute. Add the garlic and fry for a few seconds, then add the mushrooms and 2 tablespoons of the stock. Stir-fry for 4 minutes. Add the cornstarch mixture and the remaining stock. Bring to a boil, stirring, then reduce the heat and simmer for 2 minutes. Transfer to a warmed serving dish.

Clean the wok and heat over a high heat. Add the remaining oil. Add the beef and stir-fry for 3 minutes. Add to the mushroom mixture and sprinkle with the cilantro. Serve immediately.

SERVES 2–3

1½ tbsp Sichuan pepper

½ tsp salt

12 oz/350 g porterhouse steak or top round steak

200 g/7 oz mixed small mushrooms, such as cremini, enoki, and buna shimeji

½ tbsp cornstarch

½ cup Spicy Beef Stock (see page 16) or beef stock

2 tsp Chinese rice wine or dry sherry

4 tsp soy sauce

3 tbsp peanut oil

1 shallot, finely chopped

1 tsp finely chopped fresh ginger

1 large garlic clove, thinly sliced

3 tbsp chopped fresh cilantro

SPICY SICHUAN PORK

Bring a pan of water to a boil and place the pork in the pan, then cover and let simmer for about 20 minutes, skimming occasionally. Let the pork cool and rest before slicing thinly.

Heat a wok over a medium–high heat, then add the oil. Stir-fry the pork slices until they begin to shrink. Stir in the chili bean sauce, then add the black beans and the red bean paste, if using. Finally, toss in the bell peppers and the remaining ingredients and stir-fry for a couple of minutes, or until the peppers have softened. Serve immediately with rice.

SERVES 4

10 oz/280 g pork belly

1 tbsp vegetable or peanut oil

1 tbsp chili bean sauce

1 tbsp fermented black beans, rinsed and lightly mashed

1 tsp sweet red bean paste (optional)

1 green bell pepper, finely sliced

1 red bell pepper, finely sliced

1 tsp sugar

1 tsp dark soy sauce

pinch of white pepper

cooked plain rice, to serve

PAD THAI

SERVES 4

8 oz/225 g thick rice noodles

2 tbsp vegetable or peanut oil

2 garlic cloves, chopped

2 fresh red chiles, seeded and
chopped

6 oz/175 g pork tenderloin, thinly
sliced

4 oz/115 g shrimp, shelled,
deveined, and chopped

8 fresh Chinese chives, snipped

2 tbsp Thai fish sauce

juice of 1 lime

2 tsp jaggery or light brown sugar

2 eggs, beaten

3 oz/85 g fresh bean sprouts

4 tbsp chopped fresh cilantro,
plus extra sprigs to garnish

¾ cup chopped unsalted peanuts,
plus extra to serve

Prepare the noodles according to the package directions. Drain
well and set aside.

Heat a wok over a medium–high heat, then add the oil. Stir-fry
the garlic, chiles, and pork for 2–3 minutes. Add the shrimp and
stir-fry for an additional 2–3 minutes.

Add the chives and noodles, then cover and cook for
1–2 minutes. Add the fish sauce, lime juice, sugar, and eggs.
Cook, stirring and tossing constantly to mix in the eggs.

Stir in the bean sprouts, cilantro, and peanuts and mix well,
then transfer to serving dishes. Scatter over some extra peanuts
and serve immediately, garnished with coriander sprigs.

PORK STIR-FRY WITH CASHEWS, LIME & MINT

Diagonally slice the pork across the grain into thin bite-size pieces. Flatten with the back of a knife blade and spread out on a plate. Using a mortar and pestle, crush the coriander seeds, peppercorns, salt, sugar, and lime rind together. Spread the mixture over both sides of the pork, pressing it in well. Let stand for 15 minutes.

Heat a wok over a high heat, then add 1 tablespoon of the oil. Stir-fry the pork for 2–3 minutes, until no longer pink. Transfer to a plate with the juices. Wipe the wok clean with paper towels.

Heat the wok over a medium–high heat, then add the remaining oil. Stir-fry the ginger and garlic for a few seconds. Add the white parts of the scallions and the bell pepper and stir-fry for 2 minutes. Add the cashew nuts and salt, then stir-fry for an additional minute.

Increase the heat, then return the pork and juices to the wok. Add the stock, lime juice, Thai fish sauce, and the green parts of the scallions. Stir-fry for 30 seconds to heat through, then sprinkle with the mint and serve.

SERVES 2

10 oz/280 g pork tenderloin

1 tsp coriander seeds

½ tsp white peppercorns

¼ tsp salt

¼ tsp sugar

juice and finely grated rind of 1 lime

2 tbsp peanut oil

1 tsp finely chopped fresh ginger

1 garlic clove, thinly sliced

3 scallions, white and green parts separated, then halved lengthwise and sliced into ¾-inch/2-cm pieces

1 small green bell pepper, seeded and thinly sliced

2 tbsp coarsely chopped cashew nuts

large pinch of salt

1 tbsp chicken stock

1 tsp Thai fish sauce

2 tbsp coarsely chopped fresh mint, to garnish

PORK BELLY ON CHINESE LEAVES

Using the tip of a very sharp knife, score the pork rind at ½-inch/1-cm intervals. Combine the marinade ingredients, then pour the mixture into a shallow dish in which the pork will fit in a single layer. Add the pork, rubbing the marinade into the slashes. Let stand at room temperature for 1 hour, turning occasionally.

Preheat the oven to 425°F/220°C. Line a small roasting pan with foil and put a rack in it. Reserving the marinade, place the pork on the rack, and put the pan on the top shelf of the oven. Roast for 15 minutes, then reduce the oven temperature to 350°F/180°C. Turn the pork over, and brush with the marinade. Roast for 20 minutes, then turn, brush with the marinade again and roast for an additional 20 minutes. Remove from the oven and let cool. Diagonally slice the pork into ½-inch/1-cm pieces. Put in a bowl and mix with the remaining marinade.

Heat a wok over a high heat, then add 1 tablespoon of the oil. Add the pork slices and marinade and stir-fry for 2 minutes, until the marinade is reduced and bubbling. Pour in the stock, scraping up any sediment. Stir-fry for 2 minutes, until reduced. Remove from the wok and keep warm. Wipe the wok clean with paper towels.

Heat the wok over a high heat, then add the remaining oil. Add the ginger and stir-fry for a few seconds. Add the cabbage, scallions, sugar, and salt, and stir-fry for 1 minute, until just cooked and still brightly colored.

Transfer the vegetables to a warmed serving dish. Pour the pork and juices over the top and serve immediately.

SERVES 2

- 4 strips boneless pork belly, about 1 lb 7 oz/650 g in total
- 2 tbsp peanut oil
- 6 tbsp Basic Chinese Stock (see page 16) or chicken stock
- 1 thin slice fresh ginger
- ½ head Chinese cabbage, sliced diagonally into ribbons
- 6 scallions, green parts included, sliced diagonally into 1½-inch/4-cm pieces
- ½ tsp sugar
- ¼ tsp salt

marinade

- 2 tbsp sugar
- 2 tbsp Chinese rice wine or dry sherry
- 1 tbsp soy sauce
- 1½-inch/4-cm piece fresh ginger, coarsely chopped and squeezed in a garlic press
- ½ tsp salt
- ¼ tsp Chinese five-spice powder
- 4 tbsp hoisin sauce

PORK, CARROT & GINGER STIR-FRY

SERVES 2

9 oz/250 g pork tenderloin

2 tbsp peanut oil

2 large garlic cloves, thinly sliced

1 fresh green chile, seeded and
   thinly sliced diagonally

6 carrots, cut into matchstick
   strips

1½-inch/4-cm piece fresh ginger,
   cut into matchstick strips

8 oz/225 g canned bamboo
   shoots, drained

1½ tsp crushed Sichuan pepper

⅓–½ cup Basic Chinese Stock
   (see page 16) or chicken stock

2 tbsp light soy sauce

marinade

2 tsp Chinese rice wine or dry
   sherry

2 tsp light soy sauce

½ tsp sugar

¼ tsp salt

Diagonally slice the pork across the grain very thinly, then into
½ x 1½-inch/1 x 4-cm strips. Put in a bowl. Combine the marinade
ingredients and pour over the pork. Let stand for 30 minutes.

Heat a wok over a medium heat, then add the oil. Stir-fry
the garlic and chile for 30 seconds, or until the garlic just starts
to color.

Add the pork and marinade, and increase the heat to high.
Stir-fry for 1 minute, then add the carrots, ginger, bamboo shoots,
and Sichuan pepper. Stir-fry for an additional minute, then pour
in the stock and soy sauce. Stir-fry for 4–5 minutes, until the
sauce has reduced slightly. Transfer to a warmed dish and
serve immediately.

SINGAPORE NOODLES

Prepare the noodles according to the package instructions. Drain and set aside. Meanwhile, put the curry paste and turmeric in a small bowl and stir in 4 tablespoons of the water, then set aside.

Heat a wok over a high heat, then add the oil. Add the onion and garlic and stir-fry for 1 minute, or until the onion softens. Add the broccoli florets and beans to the wok with the remaining 2 tablespoons of water and continue stir-frying for 2 minutes. Add the pork and stir-fry for an additional minute. Add the shrimp, cabbage, and chile to the wok and continue stir-frying for an additional 2 minutes, until the meat is cooked through and the vegetables are tender but still have a little bite. Scoop out of the wok and keep warm.

Add the scallions, noodles, and curry paste mixture to the wok. Use 2 forks to mix the noodles and onions together, and continue stir-frying for about 2 minutes, until the noodles are hot and have picked up a dark golden color from the turmeric. Return the other ingredients to the wok and continue stir-frying and mixing for 1 minute. Garnish with fresh cilantro.

SERVES 4

7 oz/200 g fine rice noodles

1 tbsp mild, medium, or hot curry paste, to taste

1 tsp ground turmeric

6 tbsp water

2 tbsp peanut or corn oil

½ onion, thinly sliced

2 large garlic cloves, thinly sliced

½ medium head broccoli, cut into small florets

3 oz/85 g green beans, cut to 1-inch/2.5-cm lengths

3 oz/85 g pork tenderloin, cut into thin strips

3 oz/85 g cooked, shelled shrimp, thawed if frozen

⅔ cup thinly shredded Chinese cabbage or romaine lettuce

¼ Thai chile, or to taste, seeded and thinly sliced

2 scallions, white part only, thinly shredded

fresh cilantro sprigs, to garnish

HOISIN PORK WITH GARLIC NOODLES

Cook the noodles according to the package instructions. Drain well, rinse under cold running water to stop the cooking, and drain again, then set aside.

Sprinkle the pork with the sugar and use your hands to toss together. Heat a wok over a high heat, then add the peanut oil. Add the pork and stir-fry for about 3 minutes, until the pork is cooked through and is no longer pink. Use a slotted spoon to remove the pork from the wok and keep warm. Add both vinegars to the wok and boil until reduced to about 5 tablespoons. Pour in the hoisin sauce with the scallions and let simmer until reduced by half. Add to the pork and stir together.

Quickly wipe out the wok with paper towels and heat, then add the garlic-flavored oil. Add the garlic slices and stir around for about 30 seconds, until they are golden and crispy. Use a slotted spoon to scoop them out of the wok and set aside.

Add the noodles to the wok and stir to warm through. Divide the noodles among 4 serving dishes, top with the pork-and-scallion mixture, and sprinkle with the garlic slices.

SERVES 4

9 oz/250 g thick egg noodles, or whole wheat egg noodles

1 lb/450 g pork tenderloin, thinly sliced

1 tsp sugar

1 tbsp peanut or corn oil

4 tbsp rice vinegar

4 tbsp white wine vinegar

4 tbsp hoisin sauce

2 scallions, diagonally sliced

2 tbsp garlic-flavored corn oil

2 large garlic cloves, thinly sliced

ANTS CLIMBING A TREE

SERVES 4

9 oz/250 g thick rice noodles

1 tbsp cornstarch

3 tbsp soy sauce

1½ tbsp Chinese rice wine

1½ tsp sugar

1½ tsp sesame oil

12 oz/350 g lean ground pork

1½ tbsp peanut or sesame oil

2 large garlic cloves,
   finely chopped

1 large fresh red chile, or to taste,
   seeded and thinly sliced

3 scallions, finely chopped

finely chopped fresh cilantro,
   to garnish

Prepare the noodles according to the package instructions. Drain well and set aside.

Meanwhile, put the cornstarch in a separate large bowl, then add the soy sauce, rice wine, sugar, and sesame oil, stirring until smooth. Add the ground pork and use your hands to toss the ingredients together, without squeezing the pork. Set aside to marinate for 10 minutes.

Heat a wok over a high heat, then add the peanut oil. Add the garlic, chile, and scallions and stir around for about 30 seconds. Tip in the ground pork together with any marinade left in the bowl and stir-fry for about 5 minutes, or until the pork is no longer pink. Add the noodles and use 2 forks to mix together. Sprinkle with the chopped cilantro and serve.

JAPANESE-STYLE PORK

Diagonally slice the pork across the grain very thinly, then into
½ x 1½-inch/1 x 4-cm pieces. Put in a bowl. Combine the
marinade ingredients, stirring well to mix the honey, and pour
over the pork. Marinate for 1 hour at room temperature, or
overnight in the refrigerator. Drain the pork in a strainer set over
a bowl, reserving the marinade.

Heat a wok over a medium heat, then add the peanut oil.
Stir-fry the garlic for a few seconds, then add the beans and
stir-fry for 1 minute. Add the pork and marinade, and increase
the heat to high. Season with salt and black pepper, and stir-fry
for 4–5 minutes, or until the beans are tender and the pork is
cooked through.

Sprinkle with the sesame seeds and pour in the sesame oil,
then stir-fry for an additional 30 seconds. Transfer to a warmed
serving dish, and serve immediately.

SERVES 2

10 oz/280 g pork tenderloin

2 tbsp peanut oil

1 garlic clove, thinly sliced

4 oz/115 g green beans, cut to
    1½-inch/4-cm lengths

1½ tsp sesame seeds

½ tsp sesame oil

salt and pepper

marinade

3 tbsp shoyu or tamari
    (Japanese soy sauce)

3 tbsp mirin

finely grated rind and juice of
    ½ orange

1 tbsp honey

½ –1 fresh red chile, seeded and
    finely chopped

1 tsp finely chopped fresh ginger

¼ tsp salt

STIR-FRIED LAMB WITH ORANGE

Heat a wok without adding any oil. Add the ground lamb and dry-fry for 5 minutes, or until the meat is evenly browned. Drain away any excess fat from the wok.

Add the garlic, cumin seeds, coriander, and red onion to the wok and cook for an additional 5 minutes.

Stir in the orange rind and juice and the soy sauce, mixing until thoroughly combined. Cover, reduce the heat, and let simmer, stirring occasionally, for 15 minutes.

Remove the lid, increase the heat, and add the orange segments. Stir to mix.

Season to taste with salt and pepper and heat through for an additional 2–3 minutes. Transfer the stir-fry to warmed serving dishes and garnish with snipped chives and strips of orange zest. Serve immediately.

SERVES 4

1 lb/450 g ground lamb

2 garlic cloves, crushed

1 tsp cumin seeds

1 tsp ground coriander

1 red onion, sliced

finely grated rind and juice of
　1 orange

2 tbsp light soy sauce

1 orange, peeled and segmented

salt and pepper

snipped fresh chives and strips of
　orange zest, to garnish

LAMB WITH BLACK BEAN SAUCE

SERVES 4

1 lb/450 g lamb neck fillet or boneless leg of lamb

1 egg white, lightly beaten

4 tbsp cornstarch

1 tsp Chinese five-spice powder

3 tbsp sunflower oil

1 red onion, sliced

1 red bell pepper, seeded and sliced

1 green bell pepper, seeded and sliced

1 yellow or orange bell pepper, seeded and sliced

5 tbsp black bean sauce

cooked noodles, to serve

Using a sharp knife, slice the lamb into thin lengths.

Mix together the egg white, cornstarch, and Chinese five-spice powder. Toss the lamb in the mixture until evenly coated.

Heat a wok over high heat, then add the oil. Stir-fry the lamb for 5 minutes, or until it crispens around the edges.

Add the onion and bell peppers to the wok and cook for 5–6 minutes, or until the vegetables just begin to soften.

Stir the black bean sauce into the mixture in the wok and heat through.

Transfer to warmed serving dishes and serve immediately with cooked noodles.

MEAT

157

RED LAMB CURRY

Heat a wok over a high heat, then add the oil. Add the onion and garlic and stir-fry for 2–3 minutes, until softened. Add the lamb and stir-fry the mixture quickly until lightly browned.

Stir in the curry paste and cook for a few seconds, then add the coconut milk and sugar and bring to a boil. Reduce the heat and simmer for 15 minutes, stirring occasionally.

Stir in the bell pepper, stock, fish sauce, and lime juice, then cover and simmer for an additional 15 minutes, or until the lamb is tender.

Add the water chestnuts, cilantro, and chopped basil and season to taste with salt and pepper. Transfer to serving dishes, then garnish with basil leaves and serve with jasmine rice.

SERVES 4

2 tbsp vegetable oil

1 large onion, sliced

2 garlic cloves, crushed

1 lb 2 oz/500 g lean boneless leg of lamb

2 tbsp Thai red curry paste

$^2/_3$ cup coconut milk

1 tbsp light brown sugar

1 large red bell pepper, seeded and thickly sliced

$^1/_2$ cup lamb or beef stock

1 tbsp Thai fish sauce

2 tbsp lime juice

8 oz/225 g canned water chestnuts, drained

2 tbsp chopped fresh cilantro

2 tbsp chopped fresh basil, plus extra leaves to garnish

salt and pepper

cooked jasmine rice, to serve

LAMB & LEEK
STIR-FRY

Diagonally slice the lamb across the grain into thin bite-size pieces. Flatten with the back of a knife blade, and put in a bowl. Combine the garlic, soy sauce, rice wine, sugar, and salt. Pour the mixture over the lamb. Marinate for 1 hour at room temperature, or overnight in the refrigerator.

Mix the cornstarch to a thin paste with the Spicy Beef Stock. Heat a wok over a high heat, then add 1 tablespoon of the oil. Add the lamb and stir-fry for 1 minute, then season to taste with black pepper. Add the cornstarch paste and stir-fry for an additional minute. Remove from the wok and keep warm. Wipe the wok clean with paper towels.

Heat the wok over a high heat, then add the remaining oil. Add the leeks and chicken stock and stir-fry for 2 minutes, until just cooked and still bright green and crisp. Return the lamb to the wok and stir-fry for 30 seconds. Transfer to a warmed serving dish and serve immediately.

SERVES 2

10 oz/280 g lamb neck tenderloin

1 garlic clove, finely chopped

2 tsp soy sauce

2 tsp Chinese rice wine or dry sherry

½ tsp sugar

¼ tsp salt

½ tbsp cornstarch

3 tbsp Spicy Beef Stock (see page 16) or chicken stock

2 tbsp peanut oil

3 leeks, green parts included, sliced into 1½-inch/4-cm pieces

1 tbsp chicken stock or water

black pepper

XINJIANG LAMB CASSEROLE

SERVES 5–6

1–2 tbsp vegetable or peanut oil

14 oz/400 g lamb or mutton,
   cut into bite-size cubes

1 onion, coarsely chopped

1 green bell pepper, seeded and
   coarsely chopped

1 carrot, coarsely chopped

1 turnip, coarsely chopped

2 tomatoes, coarsely chopped

1-inch/2.5-cm piece fresh ginger,
   thinly sliced

1¼ cups water

1 tsp salt

Heat a wok over a high heat, then add the oil. Stir-fry the lamb for 1–2 minutes, or until the meat is sealed on all sides.

Transfer the meat to a large flameproof casserole and add all the other ingredients. Bring to a boil, then cover and let simmer over low heat for 35 minutes, until the lamb and vegetables are tender. Serve immediately.

LAMB WITH LIME LEAVES

Using a sharp knife, cut the lamb into thin strips or cubes. Set aside until required.

Heat a wok over a high heat, then add the oil. Add the garlic, shallots, lemongrass, lime leaves, tamarind paste, sugar, and chiles to the wok and stir-fry for 2 minutes.

Add the lamb to the wok and stir-fry for 5 minutes, tossing well so that the lamb is evenly coated in the spice mixture.

Pour the coconut milk into the wok and bring to a boil. Reduce the heat and let simmer for 20 minutes.

Add the cherry tomatoes and chopped cilantro to the wok and simmer for 5 minutes. Transfer to serving dishes and serve with cooked fragrant rice.

SERVES 4

1 lb/450 g lean boneless lamb (leg or loin fillet)

2 tbsp peanut oil

2 garlic cloves, crushed

4 shallots, chopped

2 lemongrass stalks, sliced

6 fresh kaffir lime leaves

1 tbsp tamarind paste

2 tbsp jaggery or light brown sugar

2 fresh red Thai chiles, seeded and finely chopped

2½ cups coconut milk

6 oz/175 g cherry tomatoes, halved

1 tbsp chopped fresh cilantro

cooked Thai fragrant rice, to serve

POULTRY

SWEET & SOUR CHICKEN

Combine all the marinade ingredients in a bowl and marinate the chicken for at least 20 minutes.

To make the sauce, heat the vinegar in a pan and add the sugar, soy sauce, and ketchup. Stir to dissolve the sugar, then set aside.

Heat a wok over a high heat, then add 3 tablespoons of the oil. Stir-fry the chicken until it starts to turn golden brown. Remove and set aside. Wipe the wok clean with paper towels.

Heat the wok over a high heat, then add the remaining oil. Cook the garlic and ginger until fragrant. Add the vegetables and cook for 2 minutes. Add the chicken and cook for 1 minute. Finally, add the sauce and sesame oil, then stir in the scallion and serve with rice.

SERVES 4–6

1 lb/450 g lean chicken, cubed

5 tbsp vegetable or peanut oil

½ tsp minced garlic

½ tsp finely chopped fresh ginger

1 green bell pepper, seeded and cut into 1-inch/2.5-cm chunks

1 onion, coarsely chopped

1 carrot, finely sliced

1 tsp sesame oil

1 tbsp finely chopped scallion

cooked plain rice, to serve

marinade

2 tsp light soy sauce

1 tsp Chinese rice wine

pinch of white pepper

½ tsp salt

dash of sesame oil

sauce

8 tbsp rice vinegar

4 tbsp sugar

2 tsp light soy sauce

6 tbsp ketchup

GONG BAU CHICKEN

Combine all the marinade ingredients in a bowl and marinate the chicken, covered, for at least 20 minutes. Combine all the sauce ingredients in a separate bowl and set aside.

Heat the wok over a high heat, then add the vegetable oil. Stir-fry the chiles and peppers until crisp and fragrant. Toss in the chicken pieces. When they begin to color, add the garlic, ginger, and scallion. Stir-fry for about 5 minutes, or until the chicken is cooked through.

Pour in the sauce and mix together thoroughly, then stir in the peanuts. Serve immediately with rice.

SERVES 4

2 skinless, boneless chicken breasts, cut into cubes

1 tbsp vegetable or peanut oil

10 dried red chiles or to taste, each snipped into 2–3 pieces

1 tsp Sichuan peppers

3 garlic cloves, finely sliced

1-inch/2.5-cm piece fresh ginger, finely sliced

1 tbsp coarsely chopped scallion, white part only

generous ½ cup roasted peanuts

cooked plain rice, to serve

marinade

2 tsp light soy sauce

1 tsp Chinese rice wine

½ tsp sugar

sauce

1 tsp light soy sauce

1 tsp dark soy sauce

1 tsp black Chinese rice vinegar

a few drops of sesame oil

2 tbsp chicken stock

1 tsp sugar

CHICKEN WITH CASHEW NUTS

SERVES 4–6

1 lb/450 g skinless, boneless chicken breast, cut into bite-size pieces

3 dried Chinese mushrooms, soaked in warm water for 20 minutes

2 tbsp vegetable or peanut oil

4 slices of fresh ginger

1 tsp finely chopped garlic

1 red bell pepper, seeded and cut into 1-inch/2.5-cm chunks

generous ½ cup roasted cashew nuts

marinade

3 tbsp light soy sauce

1 tsp Chinese rice wine

pinch of sugar

½ tsp salt

Marinate the chicken in 2 tablespoons of the soy sauce, the rice wine, sugar, and salt for at least 20 minutes.

Squeeze any excess water from the mushrooms and finely slice, discarding any tough stems. Reserve the soaking water.

Heat a wok over a medium–high heat, then add 1 tablespoon of the oil. Add the ginger and stir-fry until fragrant. Stir in the chicken and cook for 2 minutes, or until it begins to turn brown. Before the chicken is cooked through, remove and set aside. Wipe the wok clean with paper towels.

Heat the wok over a medium–high heat, then add the remaining oil. Stir-fry the garlic until fragrant. Add the mushrooms and bell pepper and stir-fry for 1 minute. Add 2 tablespoons of the mushroom soaking water and cook for about 2 minutes, or until the water has evaporated.

Return the chicken to the wok, then add the remaining soy sauce and the cashew nuts and stir-fry for 2 minutes, or until the chicken is cooked through. Serve immediately.

CHICKEN & PEANUT CURRY

Heat a wok over a medium–high heat, then add the oil. Stir-fry the onions for 1 minute. Add the curry paste and stir-fry for 1–2 minutes.

Pour in the coconut milk and stock. Add the lime leaves and lemongrass and let simmer for 1 minute. Add the chicken and gradually bring to a boil. Let simmer for 8–10 minutes, until the chicken is tender.

Stir in the fish sauce, soy sauce, and sugar and let simmer for 1–2 minutes. Stir in the peanuts, pineapple, and cucumber and cook for 30 seconds. Serve immediately with extra nuts and cucumber on the side.

SERVES 4

1 tbsp vegetable or peanut oil

2 red onions, sliced

2 tbsp Penang curry paste

1¾ cups coconut milk

⅔ cup chicken stock

4 kaffir lime leaves, coarsely torn

1 lemongrass stalk, finely chopped

6 skinless, boneless chicken thighs, chopped

1 tbsp Thai fish sauce

2 tbsp Thai soy sauce

1 tsp jaggery or light brown sugar

½ cup chopped, unsalted roasted peanuts, plus extra to serve

6 oz/175 g fresh pineapple, coarsely chopped

6-inch/15-cm piece cucumber, peeled and halved lengthwise, then seeded and sliced, plus extra to serve

CHICKEN CHOW MEIN

Prepare the noodles according to the package directions. Drain and set aside.

Meanwhile, heat a wok over a medium heat, then add the sunflower oil. Add the chicken, garlic, bell pepper, mushrooms, scallions, and bean sprouts to the wok and stir-fry for about 5 minutes.

Add the noodles to the wok, toss well, and stir-fry for an additional 5 minutes. Drizzle over the soy sauce and sesame oil and toss until thoroughly combined.

Transfer to warmed serving dishes and serve immediately.

SERVES 4

9 oz/250 g medium egg noodles

2 tbsp sunflower oil

10 oz/280 g cooked chicken breasts, shredded

1 garlic clove, finely chopped

1 red bell pepper, seeded and thinly sliced

3½ oz/100 g shiitake mushrooms, sliced

6 scallions, sliced

3½ oz/100 g fresh bean sprouts

3 tbsp soy sauce

1 tbsp sesame oil

THAI GREEN CHICKEN CURRY

SERVES 4

1 tbsp vegetable or peanut oil

1 onion, sliced

1 garlic clove, finely chopped

2–3 tbsp Thai green curry paste

1¾ cups coconut milk

⅔ cup chicken stock

4 kaffir lime leaves

4 skinless, boneless chicken
  breasts, cut into cubes

1 tbsp Thai fish sauce

2 tbsp Thai soy sauce

grated rind and juice of ½ lime

1 tsp jaggery or light brown sugar

4 tbsp chopped fresh cilantro,
  to garnish

Heat a wok over a medium–high heat, then add the oil. Stir-fry the onion and garlic for 1–2 minutes, until starting to soften. Add the curry paste and stir-fry for 1–2 minutes.

Add the coconut milk, stock, and lime leaves, bring to a boil, and add the chicken. Reduce the heat and let simmer gently for 15–20 minutes, until the chicken is tender.

Add the fish sauce, soy sauce, lime rind and juice, and sugar. Cook for 2–3 minutes, until the sugar has dissolved. Serve immediately, garnished with chopped cilantro.

THAI RED CHICKEN CURRY

Place the garlic, chiles, lemongrass, lime rind, lime leaves, curry paste, and coriander seeds in a food processor and process until the mixture is smooth.

Heat a wok over a high heat, then add the oil. Add the chicken and the garlic mixture and stir-fry for 5 minutes. Add the coconut milk, stock, and soy sauce and bring to a boil. Reduce the heat and cook, stirring, for an additional 3 minutes. Stir in the ground peanuts and let simmer for 20 minutes.

Add the scallions, bell pepper, and eggplants and let simmer, stirring occasionally, for an additional 10 minutes. Remove from the heat and stir in the cilantro. Serve immediately with cooked jasmine rice, garnished with extra cilantro.

SERVES 4

6 garlic cloves, chopped

2 fresh red chiles, chopped

2 tbsp chopped fresh lemongrass

1 tsp finely grated lime rind

1 tbsp chopped fresh kaffir lime leaves

1 tbsp Thai red curry paste

1 tbsp toasted and crushed coriander seeds

1 tbsp chili oil

4 skinless, boneless chicken breasts, sliced

1¼ cups coconut milk

1¼ cups chicken stock

1 tbsp soy sauce

⅓ cup toasted and ground unsalted peanuts

3 scallions, diagonally sliced

1 red bell pepper, seeded and sliced

3 Thai eggplants, sliced

2 tbsp chopped fresh cilantro, plus extra to garnish

cooked jasmine rice, to serve

CHICKEN FRIED RICE

Heat a wok over a medium heat, then add the oil. Add the shallots and cook until softened, then add the chicken and 2 tablespoons of the soy sauce and stir-fry for 5–6 minutes.

Stir in the carrots, celery, bell pepper, peas, and corn and stir-fry for an additional 5 minutes. Add the rice and stir thoroughly.

Finally, stir in the scrambled eggs and the remaining soy sauce. Serve immediately.

SERVES 4

½ tbsp sesame oil

6 shallots, peeled and quartered

1 lb/450g cooked chicken, diced

3 tbsp light soy sauce

2 carrots, diced

1 celery stalk, diced

1 red bell pepper, seeded and diced

1½ cups fresh peas

3½ oz/100 g canned corn kernels, drained

4 cups cooked long-grain rice

2 large eggs, scrambled

EGG FRIED RICE WITH CHICKEN

SERVES 4

generous 1 cup jasmine rice

3 skinless, boneless chicken breasts, cut into cubes

1¾ cups coconut milk

1¾ oz/50 g creamed coconut, chopped

2–3 cilantro roots, chopped

thinly pared rind of 1 lemon

1 fresh green chile, seeded and chopped

3 fresh Thai basil leaves

1 tbsp Thai fish sauce

1 tbsp oil

3 eggs, beaten

fresh chives, to garnish

fresh cilantro sprigs, to garnish

Cook the rice in a saucepan of boiling water for 12–15 minutes. Drain well, then let cool and chill overnight.

Put the chicken into a pan and cover with the coconut milk. Add the creamed coconut, cilantro roots, lemon rind, and chile and bring to a boil. Let simmer for 8–10 minutes, until the chicken is tender. Remove from the heat. Stir in the basil and fish sauce.

Meanwhile, heat a wok over a medium–high heat, then add the oil. Stir-fry the rice for 2–3 minutes. Pour in the eggs and stir until they have cooked and thoroughly mixed with the rice.

Line 4 small ovenproof bowls or ramekins with plastic wrap and pack with the rice. Turn out carefully onto serving plates and remove the plastic wrap. Garnish with chives and cilantro sprigs. Serve with the chicken mixture.

PEPPERED CHICKEN STIR-FRY

In a small bowl, combine half of the soy sauce, the cornstarch, rice wine, and salt.

Put the chicken pieces in a shallow dish and pour over the soy sauce mixture, stirring to coat. Let stand for 15 minutes.

Mix the remaining soy sauce with the stock and oyster sauce and set aside.

Heat a wok over a high heat, then add the oil. Add the chicken and stir-fry for 3 minutes, until no longer pink. Remove from the wok with a slotted spoon and drain on paper towels.

Reduce the heat slightly, then add the ginger, garlic, white scallion, and crushed peppercorns and stir for a few seconds. Add the baby corn, bell pepper, and water chestnuts. Stir-fry for 2 minutes, then return the chicken to the wok. Add the snow peas and the soy sauce mixture and stir-fry for 1–2 minutes, until the sauce is thickened.

Sprinkle with the sliced green scallion, and cook for a few more seconds. Serve immediately.

SERVES 4–6

4 tsp soy sauce

1 tbsp cornstarch

1 tbsp Chinese rice wine or dry sherry

¼ tsp salt

12 oz/350 g skinless, boneless chicken breasts, cut into cubes

6 tbsp Basic Chinese Stock (see page 16) or chicken stock

1 tbsp oyster sauce

4 tbsp peanut oil

1 tsp finely chopped fresh ginger

1 large garlic clove, thinly sliced

4 scallions, white and green parts separated, diagonally sliced into ¾-inch/2-cm pieces

½ tbsp crushed white peppercorns

8 baby corn, halved diagonally

½ small red bell pepper, seeded and thinly sliced

8 oz/225 g canned water chestnuts, drained

4 oz/115 g snow peas, halved diagonally

GINGER CHICKEN WITH SESAME SEEDS

Combine the marinade ingredients in a bowl. Add the chicken and toss to coat well. Cover with plastic wrap and let chill in the refrigerator for 1 hour.

Remove the chicken from the marinade with a slotted spoon. Heat a wok over a medium–high heat, then add the oil. Stir-fry the chicken and leek until the chicken is browned and the leek begins to soften. Stir in the remaining vegetables, the ginger, and wine. Reduce the heat, cover, and let simmer for 5 minutes.

Place the sesame seeds on a cookie sheet under a hot broiler. Stir them once to make sure they toast evenly. Set aside to cool.

In a small bowl, combine the cornstarch with the water and whisk until smooth. Gradually add the liquid to the wok, stirring constantly until thickened.

Sprinkle with the sesame seeds and serve immediately.

SERVES 4

1 lb 2 oz/500 g skinless, boneless chicken breasts, cut into strips

2 tbsp peanut oil

1 leek, thinly sliced

1 head broccoli, cut into small florets

2 carrots, thinly sliced

½ head cauliflower, cut into small florets

1 tsp grated fresh ginger

5 tbsp white wine

2 tbsp sesame seeds

1 tbsp cornstarch

1 tbsp water

marinade

4 tbsp soy sauce

4 tbsp water

CHICKEN & GREEN VEGETABLES

SERVES 4

- 9 oz/250 g medium egg noodles
- 2 tbsp peanut or corn oil
- 1 large garlic clove, crushed
- 1 fresh green chile, seeded and sliced
- 1 tbsp Chinese five-spice powder
- 2 skinless, boneless chicken breasts, cut into thin strips
- 2 green bell peppers, seeded and sliced
- 1 small head broccoli, cut into florets
- 2 oz/55 g green beans, cut into 1½-inch/4-cm pieces
- 5 tbsp vegetable or chicken stock
- 2 tbsp oyster sauce
- 2 tbsp soy sauce
- 1 tbsp Chinese rice wine or dry sherry
- 3½ oz/100 g fresh bean sprouts

Cook the noodles according to the package instructions. Drain, rinse, and drain again, then set aside.

Heat a wok over a high heat, then add 1 tablespoon of the oil. Add the garlic, chile, and five-spice powder and stir-fry for about 30 seconds. Add the chicken and stir-fry for 3 minutes, or until it is cooked through. Use a slotted spoon to remove the chicken from the wok and set aside.

Add the remaining oil to the wok and heat. Add the bell peppers, broccoli, and beans and stir-fry for about 2 minutes. Stir in the stock, oyster sauce, soy sauce, and rice wine and return the chicken to the wok. Continue stir-frying for about 1 minute, until the chicken is warmed through and the vegetables are tender but still firm to the bite. Add the noodles and bean sprouts and use 2 forks to mix all the ingredients together. Serve immediately.

191

SWEET & SOUR NOODLES WITH CHICKEN

Cook the noodles according to the package instructions. Drain, rinse, and drain again, then set aside.

Meanwhile, to make the sauce, stir half the water into the arrowroot and set aside. Mix the remaining sauce ingredients and the remaining water together in a small pan and bring to a boil. Stir in the arrowroot mixture and continue boiling until the sauce becomes clear, glossy, and thick. Remove from the heat and set aside.

Heat a wok over a high heat, then add the oil. Add the onion and stir-fry for 1 minute. Stir in the chicken, carrot, and bell pepper and continue stir-frying for about 3 minutes, or until the chicken is cooked through. Add the bamboo shoots and cashew nuts and stir them around to lightly brown the nuts.

Stir the sauce into the wok and heat until it starts to simmer. Add the noodles and use 2 forks to mix them with the chicken and vegetables. Serve immediately.

SERVES 4

9 oz/250 g medium egg noodles

2 tbsp peanut or corn oil

1 onion, thinly sliced

4 skinless, boneless chicken thighs, cut into thin strips

1 carrot, halved lengthwise and cut into thin slices

1 red bell pepper, seeded and finely chopped

4 oz/115 g canned bamboo shoots, drained

generous ½ cup cashew nuts

sweet & sour sauce

½ cup water

1½ tsp arrowroot

4 tbsp rice vinegar

3 tbsp light brown sugar

2 tsp dark soy sauce

2 tsp tomato paste

2 large garlic cloves, finely chopped

½-inch/1-cm piece fresh ginger, finely chopped

pinch of salt

YAKI SOBA

Cook the noodles according to the package instructions. Drain well and tip into a bowl.

Mix the onion, bean sprouts, bell pepper, chicken, and shrimp together in a separate bowl. Stir through the noodles.

Heat a wok over a high heat, then add the peanut oil. Add the noodle mixture and stir-fry for 4 minutes, or until golden, then add the shoyu, mirin, and sesame oil and toss together.

Divide the mixture between 2 plates, sprinkle with the sesame seeds and scallions, and serve immediately.

SERVES 2

14 oz/400 g ramen noodles

1 onion, finely sliced

7 oz/200 g fresh bean sprouts

1 red bell pepper, seeded and thinly sliced

1 boneless, skin-on cooked chicken breast, about 5½ oz/150 g, sliced

12 cooked, shelled shrimp

1 tbsp peanut oil

2 tbsp shoyu (Japanese soy sauce)

½ tbsp mirin

1 tsp sesame oil

1 tsp toasted sesame seeds

2 scallions, finely sliced

SERVES 4

peanut or corn oil, for deep-frying

9 oz/250 g fresh fine or medium
   egg noodles

chicken lime salad

6 tbsp sour cream

6 tbsp mayonnaise

1-inch/2.5-cm piece fresh ginger,
   grated

grated rind and juice of 1 lime

4 skinless, boneless chicken
   thighs, poached and cooled,
   then cut into thin strips

1 carrot, grated

1 cucumber, cut in half lengthwise,
   seeded, and sliced

1 tbsp finely chopped fresh
   cilantro

1 tbsp finely chopped
   fresh mint

1 tbsp finely chopped
   fresh parsley

salt and pepper

NOODLE BASKETS WITH CHICKEN SALAD

To shape the noodle baskets, you will need a special set of
2 long-handled wire baskets that clip inside each other, available
from specialty kitchen stores. Dip the larger wire basket in
oil, then line it completely and evenly with one quarter of the
noodles. Dip the smaller wire basket in oil, then position it inside
the larger basket and clip it into position.

   Heat the oil in a wok to 350°F/180°C, or until a cube of bread
browns in 30 seconds. Lower the baskets into the oil and deep-fry
for 2–3 minutes, or until the noodles are golden brown. Remove
the baskets from the oil and drain on paper towels. Unclip the
2 wire baskets and carefully remove the small one. Use a palette
knife, if necessary, to pry the noodle basket from the wire frame.
Repeat to make 3 more baskets. Set aside to cool.

   To make the salad, combine the sour cream, mayonnaise,
ginger, and lime rind. Gradually add the lime juice until you get
the flavor you like. Stir in the chicken, carrot, and cucumber and
season to taste with salt and pepper. Cover and let chill.

   To serve, stir in the herbs and spoon the salad into the
noodle baskets.

TURKEY WITH MUSHROOMS & ZUCCHINI

To make the marinade, combine the sherry, lemon juice, soy sauce, ginger, and garlic in a bowl. Add the turkey and stir until coated well. Cover with plastic wrap and let marinate in the refrigerator for 3–4 hours.

Heat a wok over high heat, then add the oil. Remove the turkey from the marinade with a slotted spoon and reserve the marinade. Stir-fry a few pieces at a time until browned. Remove the turkey from the wok and set aside.

Add the mushrooms, bell pepper, and zucchini to the wok and stir-fry for 3 minutes. Add the scallions and stir-fry for an additional minute. Add the bamboo shoots and water chestnuts to the wok, then add the turkey along with half of the reserved marinade. Stir over medium–high heat for an additional 2–3 minutes, or until the ingredients are evenly coated and the marinade has reduced.

Serve immediately in warmed dishes with lemon wedges for squeezing over.

SERVES 4

1 lb/450 g turkey breast, cubed

1 tbsp sesame oil

10 small mushrooms, halved

1 green bell pepper, seeded and thinly sliced

1 zucchini, halved and thinly sliced

4 scallions, quartered

4 oz/115 g canned bamboo shoots, drained

4 oz/115 g canned water chestnuts, drained and sliced

lemon wedges, to serve

marinade

4 tbsp sweet sherry

1 tbsp lemon juice

1 tbsp light soy sauce

2 tsp grated fresh ginger

1 garlic clove, crushed

TURKEY TERIYAKI

Mix the glaze ingredients in a small saucepan over a low–medium heat. Stir until the honey has melted, then remove from the heat and let cool.

Put the turkey in a large shallow dish. Pour over the glaze, turning the pieces so they are well coated. Marinate for 30 minutes at room temperature, or overnight in the refrigerator.

Using a slotted spoon, remove the turkey from the marinade, shaking off the excess liquid. Reserve the marinade.

Heat a wok over a medium–high heat, then add the oil. Add the turkey and stir-fry for 2 minutes. Add the bell pepper and scallions, and stir-fry for 1 minute. Pour in the reserved marinade. Bring to a boil, then reduce the heat slightly and cook for 3–4 minutes, until the turkey is cooked through.

Transfer the turkey and vegetables to a warmed serving dish. Boil the liquid remaining in the wok until syrupy, then pour over the turkey. Serve immediately with rice.

SERVES 4

1 lb/450 g turkey steaks, cut into thin pieces

3 tbsp peanut oil

1 small yellow bell pepper, seeded and thinly sliced

8 scallions, green parts included, diagonally sliced into 1-inch/ 2.5-cm pieces

cooked plain rice, to serve

teriyaki glaze

5 tbsp shoyu (Japanese soy sauce)

5 tbsp mirin

2 tbsp honey

1 tsp finely chopped fresh ginger

TURKEY WITH BOK CHOY & MUSHROOMS

SERVES 4

8 oz/225 g medium egg noodles

3 tbsp peanut oil

1 large garlic clove, thinly sliced

2 tsp finely chopped fresh ginger

1 lb/450 g turkey steaks, cut into thin pieces

6 oz/175 g cremini mushrooms, thinly sliced

1 lb 5 oz/600 g bok choy, stalks chopped into 1-inch/2.5-cm pieces, leaves sliced into wide ribbons

4 scallions, green parts included, diagonally sliced into 1-inch/ 2.5-cm pieces

1 tbsp light soy sauce

2 tbsp chopped fresh cilantro

salt and pepper

Cook the noodles according to the package directions. Drain, rinse, and drain again, then let cool.

Heat a wok over a medium–high heat, then add the oil. Stir-fry the garlic and ginger for a few seconds to flavor the oil.

Add the turkey and stir-fry for 2 minutes, until no longer pink. Add the mushrooms and bok choy stalks, and stir-fry for 2 minutes. Add the bok choy leaves and the scallions, and stir-fry for an additional 2 minutes. Stir in the noodles and soy sauce, and season to taste with salt and black pepper. Cook until the noodles are heated through, then add the cilantro. Serve immediately.

TURKEY WITH HOISIN SAUCE & CASHEW NUTS

To make the marinade, mix the cornstarch and rice wine to a paste. Add the pepper, salt, egg white, and sesame oil, mixing well. Put the turkey in a shallow dish, and add the marinade, turning to coat well. Let stand for 30 minutes.

Heat a wok, preferably nonstick, over a high heat, then add 3 tablespoons of the peanut oil. Add the garlic and white parts of the scallions, and stir for a few seconds to flavor the oil. Add the turkey and reduce the heat slightly. Stir-fry for 2 minutes, until no longer pink, then sprinkle with the rice wine. Transfer to a plate with a slotted spoon.

Increase the heat to high, then add the remaining peanut oil. Swirl the oil around the wok, then stir in the hoisin sauce. Return the turkey mixture to the wok and stir-fry for 2–3 minutes, turning to coat, until cooked through.

Add the cashew nuts and green parts of the scallions. Transfer to a warmed serving dish, and serve immediately.

SERVES 4

1 lb/450 g turkey steaks, cubed

4 tbsp peanut oil

3 large garlic cloves, thinly sliced

4 scallions, white and green parts separated, diagonally sliced into ³⁄₄-inch/2-cm pieces

1 tbsp Chinese rice wine or dry sherry

3 tbsp hoisin sauce

4 tbsp cashew nuts

marinade

1 tsp cornstarch

1 tbsp Chinese rice wine or dry sherry

¹⁄₄ tsp white pepper

¹⁄₂ tsp salt

¹⁄₂ egg white, lightly beaten

2 tsp sesame oil

FRUITY DUCK
STIR-FRY

Using a sharp knife, cut the duck into thin slices.

Mix together the Chinese five-spice powder and cornstarch. Toss the duck in the mixture until well coated.

Heat a wok over a high heat, then add the oil. Cook the duck for 10 minutes, or until just beginning to crispen around the edges. Remove from the wok and set aside.

Add the onions and garlic to the wok and cook for 5 minutes, or until softened. Add the baby corn and cook for an additional 5 minutes. Add the pineapple, scallions, and bean sprouts and cook for 3–4 minutes. Stir in the plum sauce.

Return the cooked duck to the wok and toss until well mixed. Transfer to warmed serving dishes and serve hot.

SERVES 4

4 skinless, boneless duck breasts

1 tsp Chinese five-spice powder

1 tbsp cornstarch

1 tbsp chili oil

8 oz/225 g pearl onions, peeled

2 garlic cloves, crushed

3½ oz/100 g baby corn

14 oz/400 g canned pineapple
   chunks, drained

6 scallions, sliced

4 oz/115 g fresh bean sprouts

2 tbsp plum sauce

THREE-PEA STIR-FRY WITH DUCK

SERVES 4

1 lb/450 g skinless, boneless duck breasts

3 tbsp peanut oil

6 large scallions, white and green parts separated, diagonally sliced into ¾-inch/2-cm pieces

1 tsp finely chopped fresh ginger

6 oz/175 g sugar snap peas

4 oz/115 g snow peas, diagonally sliced in half

1⅓ cups shelled peas

3 tbsp whole almonds with skin, halved lengthwise

2 oz/55 g fresh bean sprouts

cooked noodles, to serve

marinade

1 tbsp light brown sugar

3 tbsp warmed water

1–2 fresh red chiles, seeded and finely chopped

1 tbsp soy sauce

1 tsp Thai fish sauce

3 tbsp lime juice

Combine the marinade ingredients in a bowl, stirring to dissolve the sugar. Slice the duck into bite-size pieces and add to the marinade. Marinate at room temperature for 30 minutes, or overnight in the refrigerator.

Heat a wok over a high heat, then add the oil. Stir-fry the white parts of the scallions and the ginger for a few seconds. Add the duck and the marinade, and stir-fry for about 5 minutes. When the liquid has reduced slightly, add the three types of pea, and stir-fry for another 2–3 minutes.

Add the almonds, bean sprouts, and green parts of the scallions, and stir-fry for a few seconds to heat through. Serve with the cooked noodles.

DUCK WITH MIXED PEPPERS

Heat a wok over a high heat, then add the oil. Cook the duck breasts, skin-side down, for 5–10 minutes, until crispy and brown. Turn over and cook for another 5 minutes, until cooked through. Remove the duck from the wok and keep warm.

Pour off any excess fat and stir-fry the onion and garlic for 2–3 minutes, until softened and lightly browned.

Add the bell peppers and stir-fry for 2–3 minutes, until tender. Add the tomatoes, stock, and soy sauce, and let simmer for 1–2 minutes. Transfer to a serving plate. Slice the duck thickly and arrange on top, spooning any sauce over it. Serve with cooked noodles.

SERVES 4

1 tbsp vegetable or peanut oil

2 boneless duck breasts, skin on

1 onion, sliced

2 garlic cloves, chopped

1 red bell pepper, seeded and sliced

1 green bell pepper, seeded and sliced

1 yellow bell pepper, seeded and sliced

4 tomatoes, peeled, seeded, and chopped

²/₃ cup stock

3 tbsp Thai soy sauce

cooked noodles, sprinkled with chopped scallion, to serve

DUCK WITH BLACK BEANS & BROCCOLI

Remove and discard the skin from the duck. Slice the meat into ¼-inch/5-mm strips.

Soak the beans in cold water for 30 minutes, then drain.

In a small bowl, combine the soy sauce, vinegar, and sugar, stirring to dissolve the sugar.

Divide the broccoli into florets. Slice the stems thinly, and slice the florets into pieces no more than ¾ inch/2 cm wide.

Heat a wok over a medium heat, then add the oil. Fry the ginger, chile, and garlic for a few seconds to flavor the oil. Add the drained beans, broccoli, and bell pepper. Increase the heat to high and stir-fry for 2 minutes.

Add the duck and stir-fry for 2 minutes, then add the soy sauce mixture. Continue to stir-fry for an additional 2 minutes. Serve immediately.

SERVES 2–3

- 2 small duck breasts, weighing 1 lb/450 g in total
- 2 tbsp salted black beans
- 1½ tbsp soy sauce
- 1 tbsp rice vinegar
- 2 tsp sugar
- 1 medium head broccoli
- 3 tbsp peanut oil
- 2.5-cm/1-inch piece fresh ginger, cut into thin shreds
- 1 fresh red chile, seeded and thinly sliced diagonally
- 1 large garlic clove, thinly sliced
- ½ red bell pepper, seeded and thinly sliced

CANTONESE SWEET & SOUR DUCK

SERVES 6

2 duck breasts, weighing about
1 lb 4 oz/550 g in total

½ tbsp soy sauce

2 tsp peanut oil

salt and pepper

1½-inch/4-cm piece of cucumber,
peeled and sliced lengthwise
into matchsticks, to garnish

sauce

1 tbsp cornstarch

½ cup Basic Chinese Stock
(see page 16) or chicken stock

1½ tbsp soy sauce

1½ tbsp rice vinegar

2 tbsp sugar

1 tbsp tomato paste

1 tbsp orange juice

2 tsp peanut oil

3 thin slices fresh ginger

Slice each duck breast into 3 pieces and put in a dish. Rub with salt and pepper and the ½ tablespoon of soy sauce.

Heat a wok over a medium–high heat, then add the oil. Fry the duck for 6 minutes, starting with the skin-side down and turning until brown and crisp on all sides. Using tongs, transfer to a plate, and let rest in a warm place for 10 minutes. Discard the oil and wipe the wok clean with paper towels. Slice the duck into ½-inch/1-cm strips (the meat will still be rare at this stage).

To prepare the sauce, mix the cornstarch to a smooth paste with 3 tablespoons of the stock. In a small bowl, combine the soy sauce, vinegar, and sugar, stirring to dissolve the sugar. Add the tomato paste and orange juice, mixing well.

Heat a clean wok over a medium heat, then add the oil. Add the ginger slices and stir-fry for a few seconds to flavor the oil. Add the soy sauce mixture and the remaining stock and bring to a boil. Reduce the heat slightly and add the cornstarch paste. Stir until starting to thicken, then add the duck slices, stirring to coat with the sauce. Simmer over a low heat for 5 minutes, until the duck is cooked but still slightly pink.

Remove the ginger slices, and transfer the duck and sauce to a warmed serving dish. Garnish with the cucumber and serve immediately.

FISH & SEAFOOD

CHILES STUFFED WITH FISH PASTE

Combine all the ingredients for the marinade in a bowl and marinate the fish for 20 minutes. Add the egg and mix by hand to create a smooth paste.

To prepare the chiles, cut in half lengthwise and scoop out the seeds and loose flesh. Cut into bite-size pieces. Spread each piece of chile with about ½ teaspoon of the fish paste.

Heat a wok over a medium–high heat, then add the oil. Cook the chile pieces on both sides until beginning to turn golden brown. Drain and set aside.

Heat a clean wok over a medium–high heat, then add 1 tablespoon of the oil. Stir-fry the garlic until aromatic. Stir in the black beans and mix well. Add the light soy sauce and sugar and stir, then add the chile pieces. Add the water, then cover and let simmer over low heat for 5 minutes. Serve immediately.

SERVES 4–6

8 oz/225 g white fish, minced

2 tbsp lightly beaten egg

4–6 mild red and green chiles

1 tbsp vegetable or peanut oil, plus extra for shallow-frying

2 garlic cloves, finely chopped

½ tsp fermented black beans, rinsed and lightly mashed

1 tbsp light soy sauce

pinch of sugar

1 tbsp water

marinade

1 tsp finely chopped fresh ginger

pinch of salt

pinch of white pepper

½ tsp vegetable or peanut oil

FRIED FISH WITH PINE NUTS

Sprinkle the salt over the fish and set aside for 20 minutes. Squeeze out any excess water from the mushrooms and finely slice, discarding any tough stems.

Heat a wok over a medium–high heat, then add 2 tablespoons of the oil. Fry the fish for 3 minutes. Drain and set aside.

Heat a clean wok over a medium–high heat, then add the remaining oil. Toss in the ginger and stir until fragrant. Add the scallions, bell peppers, bamboo shoots, mushrooms, and rice wine and cook for 1–2 minutes.

Finally, add the fish and stir to warm through. Garnish with the pine nuts and serve.

SERVES 4–6

½ tsp salt

1 lb/450 g thick white fish fillets, cut into 1-inch/2.5-cm chunks

2 dried Chinese mushrooms, soaked in warm water for 20 minutes

3 tbsp vegetable or peanut oil

1-inch/2.5-cm piece fresh ginger, finely shredded

1 tbsp chopped scallions

1 red bell pepper, seeded and cut into 1-inch/2.5-cm squares

1 green bell pepper, seeded and cut into 1-inch/2.5-cm squares

25 g/1 oz fresh or canned bamboo shoots, rinsed and cut into small cubes (if using fresh shoots, boil in water first for 30 minutes)

2 tsp Chinese rice wine

2 tbsp toasted pine nuts

STIR-FRIED RICE NOODLES WITH MARINATED FISH

SERVES 4

1 lb monkfish or cod, cut into
   1-inch/2.5-cm chunks

8 oz/225 g salmon fillets, cut into
   1-inch/2.5-cm chunks

4 tbsp vegetable or peanut oil

2 fresh green chiles, seeded and
   chopped

grated rind and juice of 1 lime

1 tbsp Thai fish sauce

4 oz/115 g thick rice noodles

2 shallots, sliced

2 garlic cloves, chopped finely

1 fresh red chile, seeded and
   chopped

2 tbsp Thai soy sauce

2 tbsp chili sauce

fresh cilantro, to garnish

Place the fish in a shallow bowl. To make the marinade, mix
2 tablespoons of the oil, the green chiles, lime juice and rind,
and fish sauce together and pour over the fish. Cover and chill for
2 hours.

Prepare the noodles according to the packet instructions. Drain
well and set aside.

Heat a wok over a medium–high heat, then add the remaining
oil. Sauté the shallots, garlic, and red chile until lightly browned.
Add the soy sauce and chili sauce. Add the fish and marinade to
the wok and stir-fry gently for 2–3 minutes, until cooked through.

Add the drained noodles and stir gently. Garnish with cilantro
and serve immediately.

FISH CURRY WITH RICE NOODLES

Heat a wok over a medium–high heat, then add the oil. Gently sauté the onion, garlic, and mushrooms until softened but not browned.

Add the fish, curry paste, and coconut milk and bring gently to a boil. Let simmer for 2–3 minutes before adding half the cilantro, the sugar, and fish sauce. Keep warm.

Meanwhile, prepare the noodles according to the package directions. Drain well through a colander. Put the colander and noodles over a pan of simmering water. Add the scallions, bean sprouts, and most of the basil and steam on top of the noodles for 1–2 minutes, or until just wilted.

Pile the noodles onto serving plates and top with the fish curry. Garnish with the remaining cilantro and basil and serve immediately.

224

SERVES 4

2 tbsp vegetable or peanut oil

1 large onion, chopped

2 garlic cloves, chopped

3 oz/75 g white mushrooms

8 oz/225 g monkfish, cut into 1-inch/2.5-cm chunks

8 oz/225 g salmon fillets, cut into 1-inch/2.5-cm chunks

8 oz/225 g cod, cut into 1-inch/2.5-cm chunks

2 tbsp Thai red curry paste

$1^{3}/_{4}$ cups coconut milk

handful of fresh cilantro, chopped

1 tsp jaggery or light brown sugar

1 tsp Thai fish sauce

4 oz/115 g rice noodles

3 scallions, chopped

3 oz/85 g fresh bean sprouts

few Thai basil leaves

MONKFISH STIR-FRY

Heat a wok over a medium–high heat, then add the oil. Add the fish, onion, garlic, ginger, asparagus, and mushrooms. Stir-fry for 2–3 minutes.

Stir in the soy sauce and lemon juice and cook for an additional minute. Remove from the heat and transfer to serving dishes. Serve immediately.

SERVES 4

2 tsp sesame oil

1 lb/450 g monkfish fillets, cut into 1-inch/2.5-cm chunks

1 onion, thinly sliced

3 garlic cloves, finely chopped

1 tsp grated fresh ginger

8 oz/225 g fine asparagus

3 cups thinly sliced mushrooms

2 tbsp light soy sauce

1 tbsp lemon juice

MONKFISH WITH LIME & CHILI SAUCE

SERVES 4

4 monkfish fillets, 4 oz/115 g each

¼ cup rice flour or cornstarch

6 tbsp vegetable or peanut oil

4 garlic cloves, crushed

2 large fresh red chiles, seeded and sliced

2 tsp jaggery or light brown sugar

juice of 2 limes

grated rind of 1 lime

2–3 tbsp water

cooked plain rice, to serve

Toss the fish in the flour, shaking off any excess. Heat a wok over a medium–high heat, then add the oil. Cook the fish on all sides until browned and cooked through, being careful when turning to avoid breaking it up.

Lift the fish out of the wok and keep warm. Add the garlic and chiles and stir-fry for 1–2 minutes, until they have softened.

Add the sugar, the lime juice and rind, and water and bring to a boil. Let simmer gently for 1–2 minutes, then spoon the mixture over the fish. Serve immediately with rice.

STEAMED SALMON WITH BOK CHOY & ASPARAGUS

Place the salmon steaks in a single layer on a heatproof plate that will fit into a wok. Combine the ginger, rice wine, soy sauce, and salt. Sprinkle this over the fish, rubbing it into the flesh. Let stand for 20 minutes, turning once.

Snap the woody ends from the asparagus and discard. Cut off the tips and reserve. Chop the stems into 2 or 3 pieces. Place a trivet in a wok with a lid, and add enough water to come halfway up the trivet. Bring to a boil, then place the plate of fish on the trivet, and cover with a loose tent of foil. Adjust the heat so the water is only just boiling. Put the lid on the wok and steam for 10–15 minutes, until the fish is opaque and just starting to flake.

Meanwhile, heat a second wok over a high heat, then add 2 tablespoons of the peanut oil. Add the asparagus stalks and bok choy, and stir-fry for 4–5 minutes, until just tender but still crisp. Splash with a good squeeze of lime juice, and season with salt and pepper. Arrange in small mounds on warmed serving plates.

Carefully lift the salmon steaks from the wok and place on top of the vegetables. Heat the sesame oil and remaining peanut oil until very hot. Add the asparagus tips and stir-fry for 20 seconds, until barely cooked. Season with black pepper. Arrange the tips on top of the fish and pour the hot oil over the top. Serve with rice.

SERVES 4

- 4 salmon steaks, about 1 inch/ 2.5 cm thick
- 2 tsp finely chopped fresh ginger
- 2 tbsp Chinese rice wine or dry sherry
- 1 tbsp light soy sauce
- ½ tsp salt
- 8 asparagus spears
- 4 tbsp peanut oil
- 3 heads bok choy, quartered lengthwise
- good squeeze of lime juice
- 2 tsp sesame oil
- black pepper
- cooked plain rice, to serve

SALMON & SCALLOPS WITH CILANTRO & LIME

Heat a wok over a medium–high heat, then add the oil. Add the salmon and scallops and stir-fry for 3 minutes. Remove from the wok, then set aside and keep warm.

Add the carrots, celery, bell peppers, mushrooms, and garlic to the wok and stir-fry for 3 minutes. Stir in the cilantro and shallots.

Add the lime juice and rind, dried red pepper flakes, sherry, and soy sauce and stir. Return the salmon and scallops to the wok and stir-fry carefully for an additional minute. Serve immediately.

SERVES 4

6 tbsp peanut oil

10 oz/280 g salmon steak, skinned and cut into 1-inch/2.5-cm chunks

8 oz/225 g prepared scallops

3 carrots, thinly sliced

2 celery stalks, cut into 1-inch/2.5-cm pieces

2 yellow bell peppers, seeded and thinly sliced

3 cups oyster mushrooms, thinly sliced

1 garlic clove, crushed

6 tbsp chopped fresh cilantro

3 shallots, thinly sliced

juice of 2 limes

1 tsp grated lime rind

1 tsp dried red pepper flakes

3 tbsp dry sherry

3 tbsp light soy sauce

SAUTÉED MACKEREL FILLETS WITH GINGER & SCALLIONS

SERVES 2–3

4 mackerel fillets with skin, weighing about 1 lb/450 g in total

1 tsp finely chopped fresh ginger, plus ¾-inch/2-cm piece finely shredded lengthwise

½ tsp salt

4 tbsp peanut oil

2½ tbsp all-purpose flour

3 scallions, green parts included, sliced

finely shredded Chinese cabbage, to garnish

sauce

2 tbsp light soy sauce

½ tsp sugar

2 tsp Chinese rice wine or dry sherry

Slice the mackerel fillets in half crosswise. Diagonally slash the skin of each piece once or twice. Combine the teaspoon of chopped ginger with the salt. Rub the mixture over both sides of the fish, rubbing it into the slashes in the flesh. Let stand for 15 minutes.

Combine the sauce ingredients in a small bowl, and set aside.

Heat a wok over a medium–high heat, then add the oil. Dredge the mackerel fillets in the flour and add to the wok. Fry for 4 minutes, turning once. Pour the sauce over the fish, sprinkle with the shredded ginger and scallions, and fry for another 2 minutes.

Transfer to a serving dish and garnish with a few shreds of Chinese cabbage. Serve immediately.

SWEET & SOUR FRIED SWORDFISH

Remove and discard the skin from the fish and slice into bite-size chunks. Spread out on a plate, and sprinkle with the salt. Sift the flour and cornstarch together to get rid of any lumps, then spread out on a second plate.

Next make the sauce. Mix the cornstarch, sugar, and rice vinegar to a smooth paste. Stir in the soy sauce, tomato paste, rice wine, orange juice, and stock. Heat a wok over a medium–high heat, then add the oil. Fry the garlic, ginger, and scallion for 1½ minutes. Add the red and green bell peppers, and stir-fry for 30 seconds. Pour in the cornstarch mixture, increase the heat slightly, and stir until thickened. Set aside.

Dip the fish in the beaten egg white, then dredge with the flour-cornstarch mixture. Heat a wok, preferably nonstick, over a medium–high heat, then add the oil and chicken stock. Add the fish and fry for 5–6 minutes, turning to cook each side. Pour in the sauce and simmer for 1–2 minutes, carefully turning the fish so it is coated with the sauce. Serve.

SERVES 2

1 lb/450 g swordfish steaks

1 tsp salt

4 tsp all-purpose flour

4 tsp cornstarch

1 egg white, lightly beaten

1½ tbsp peanut oil

3 tbsp chicken stock

sweet & sour sauce

2 tsp cornstarch

1½ tbsp sugar

1½ tbsp rice vinegar

4 tsp soy sauce

4 tsp tomato paste

4 tsp Chinese rice wine or dry sherry

3 tbsp orange juice

3 tbsp chicken stock

2 tsp vegetable oil

1 large garlic clove, crushed

1 tsp finely chopped fresh ginger

2 tbsp chopped scallion

¼ small red bell pepper, seeded and thinly sliced

¼ small green bell pepper, seeded and thinly sliced

SEAFOOD CHOW MEIN

Open up the squid and score the inside in a crisscross pattern, then cut into bite-size pieces. Soak the squid in a bowl of boiling water until all the pieces curl up. Rinse in cold water and drain.

Cut each scallop into 3–4 slices. Cut the shrimp in half lengthwise if large. Mix the scallops and shrimp with the egg white and cornstarch paste.

Cook the noodles according to the package directions. Drain and rinse under cold water. Drain well, then toss with about 1 tablespoon of oil.

Heat 3 tablespoons of oil in a preheated wok. Add the noodles and 1 tablespoon of the soy sauce and stir-fry for 2–3 minutes. Transfer to a large serving dish.

Heat the remaining oil in the wok and add the snow peas and seafood. Stir-fry for about 2 minutes, then add the salt, sugar, rice wine, the remaining soy sauce, and about half the scallions. Mix well and add a little water if necessary. Pour the seafood mixture on top of the noodles and sprinkle with sesame oil. Garnish with the remaining scallions and serve immediately.

SERVES 4

3 oz/85 g squid, cleaned

3–4 prepared scallops

3 oz/85 g shrimp, peeled and deveined

½ egg white, lightly beaten

2 tsp cornstarch, mixed to a paste with 2½ tsp water

9½ oz/275 g egg noodles

5–6 tbsp vegetable oil

2 tbsp light soy sauce

2 oz/55 g snow peas

½ tsp salt

½ tsp sugar

1 tsp Chinese rice wine

2 scallions, finely shredded

few drops of sesame oil

SPICY THAI SEAFOOD STEW

SERVES 4

7 oz/200 g squid, cleaned and tentacles discarded

1 lb 2 oz/500 g firm white fish fillet, preferably monkfish or halibut

1 tbsp corn oil

4 shallots, finely chopped

2 garlic cloves, finely chopped

2 tbsp Thai green curry paste

2 small lemongrass stalks, finely chopped

1 tsp shrimp paste

generous 2 cups coconut milk

7 oz/200 g jumbo shrimp, shelled and deveined

12 clams in shells, cleaned

8 fresh basil leaves, finely shredded

fresh basil leaves, to garnish

cooked plain rice, to serve

Using a sharp knife, cut the squid body cavities into thick rings and the white fish into bite-size chunks.

Heat a wok over a medium–high heat, then add the oil. Add the shallots, garlic, and curry paste and stir-fry for 1–2 minutes. Add the lemongrass and shrimp paste, then stir in the coconut milk and bring to a boil.

Reduce the heat until the liquid is simmering gently, then add the white fish, squid, and shrimp to the wok and simmer for 2 minutes.

Add the clams and simmer for an additional 1 minute, or until the clams have opened. Discard any clams that remain closed.

Sprinkle the shredded basil leaves over the stew. Transfer to serving plates, then garnish with whole basil leaves and serve immediately with rice.

MIXED SEAFOOD CURRY

Heat a wok over a medium–high heat, then add the oil. Stir-fry the shallots, galangal, and garlic for 1–2 minutes, until they start to soften. Add the coconut milk, lemongrass, fish sauce, and chili sauce. Bring to a boil, reduce the heat, and let simmer for 1–2 minutes.

Add the shrimp, squid, salmon, and tuna, and let simmer for 3–4 minutes, until the shrimp have turned pink and the fish is cooked.

Add the mussels and cover the wok with a lid. Let simmer for 1–2 minutes, until they have opened. Discard any mussels that remain closed. Garnish with Chinese chives and serve immediately with rice.

SERVES 4

1 tbsp vegetable or peanut oil

3 shallots, chopped finely

1-inch/2.5-cm piece fresh galangal, peeled and sliced thinly

2 garlic cloves, chopped finely

1¾ cups coconut milk

2 lemongrass stalks, snapped in half

4 tbsp Thai fish sauce

2 tbsp chili sauce

8 oz/225 g jumbo shrimp, shelled

8 oz/225 g baby squid, cleaned and sliced thickly

8 oz/225 g salmon fillet, skinned and cut into chunks

6 oz/175 g tuna steak, cut into chunks

8 oz/225 g fresh mussels, scrubbed and debearded

fresh Chinese chives, to garnish

cooked plain rice, to serve

SCALLOPS IN BLACK BEAN SAUCE

Heat a wok over a medium–high heat, then add the oil. Add the garlic and stir, then add the ginger and stir-fry together for about 1 minute, or until fragrant. Mix in the black beans, add the scallops, and stir-fry for 1 minute.

Add the soy sauce, rice wine, sugar, and chiles. Reduce the heat and simmer for 2 minutes, then add the stock. Finally, add the scallion, then stir and serve immediately.

SERVES 4

2 tbsp vegetable or peanut oil

1 tsp finely chopped garlic

1 tsp finely chopped fresh ginger

1 tbsp fermented black beans, rinsed and lightly mashed

14 oz/400 g prepared scallops

½ tsp light soy sauce

1 tsp Chinese rice wine

1 tsp sugar

3–4 fresh red Thai chiles, finely chopped

1–2 tsp chicken stock

1 tbsp finely chopped scallion

SPICY SCALLOPS WITH LIME & CHILE

SERVES 4

16 large scallops, shelled

1 tbsp butter

1 tbsp vegetable oil

1 tsp crushed garlic

1 tsp grated fresh ginger

1 bunch of scallions, finely sliced

finely grated rind of 1 lime

1 small fresh red chile, seeded and finely chopped

3 tbsp lime juice

lime wedges, to garnish

cooked plain rice, to serve

Using a sharp knife, trim the scallops to remove any black intestine, then wash and pat dry with paper towels. Separate the corals from the white parts, then slice each white part in half horizontally, making 2 circles.

Heat a wok over a medium heat, then add the butter and oil. Add the garlic and ginger and stir-fry for 1 minute without browning. Add the scallions and stir-fry for an additional minute.

Increase the heat to high, then add the scallops and continue stir-frying for 4–5 minutes. Stir in the lime rind, chile, and lime juice and cook for an additional minute.

Transfer the scallops to serving plates, then spoon over the pan juices and garnish with lime wedges. Serve hot with plain rice.

CLAMS IN BLACK BEAN SAUCE

Discard any clams with broken shells and any that refuse to close when tapped. Wash the remaining clams thoroughly and let soak in clean water until ready to cook.

Heat a wok over a medium–high heat, then add the oil. Stir-fry the ginger and garlic until fragrant. Add the black beans and cook for 1 minute.

Increase the heat to high, then add the clams and rice wine and stir-fry for 2 minutes to mix everything together. Cover and cook for about 3 minutes. Discard any clams that remain closed. Add the scallion and salt, if needed, and serve immediately.

SERVES 4

2 lb/900 g small clams

1 tbsp vegetable or peanut oil

1 tsp finely chopped fresh ginger

1 tsp finely chopped garlic

1 tbsp fermented black beans, rinsed and coarsely chopped

2 tsp Chinese rice wine

1 tbsp finely chopped scallion

1 tsp salt (optional)

STIR-FRIED FRESH CRAB WITH GINGER

Heat a wok over a medium–high heat, then add 2 tablespoons
of the oil. Cook the crab for 3–4 minutes. Remove and set aside.
Wipe the wok clean with paper towels.

In the clean wok, heat the remaining oil, then add the ginger
and stir until fragrant. Add the scallions, then stir in the crab
pieces. Add the soy sauce, sugar, and pepper. Cover and simmer
for 1 minute, then serve immediately in warmed bowls.

SERVES 4

3 tbsp vegetable or peanut oil

2 large fresh crabs, cleaned,
  broken into pieces, and legs
  cracked with a cleaver

1½-inch/4-cm piece fresh ginger,
  julienned

7 scallions, chopped into
  2-inch/5-cm lengths

2 tbsp light soy sauce

1 tsp sugar

pinch of white pepper

SCALLOP, SNOW PEAS & MUSHROOM STIR-FRY

SERVES 4

3 tbsp peanut oil

2 tbsp sesame oil

16 large scallops, halved

8 oz/225 g small shiitake
mushrooms, tough stalks
removed

6 oz/175 g snow peas, halved
diagonally

2 tsp finely chopped fresh ginger

2 garlic cloves, finely chopped

2 tsp light soy sauce

juice of 1 lime

3 tbsp torn cilantro

salt and pepper

Heat a wok over a high heat, then add the oils. Stir-fry the scallops for 1 minute. Add the mushrooms and snow peas, and stir-fry for an additional minute.

Add the ginger, garlic, and soy sauce, and a splash of water to moisten. Stir-fry for an additional 1–2 minutes, until the vegetables are just tender.

Add the lime juice and cilantro, and season to taste with salt and pepper. Divide between plates and serve at once.

MALAYSIAN-STYLE COCONUT NOODLES WITH SHRIMP

Heat a wok over a high heat, then add the oil. Add the red bell pepper, bok choy stalks, and garlic and stir-fry for 3 minutes. Add the turmeric, garam masala, chili powder, if using, and bok choy leaves, and stir-fry for 1 minute.

Mix the hot stock and peanut butter together in a heatproof bowl until the peanut butter has dissolved, then add to the stir-fry with the coconut milk and soy sauce. Reduce the heat to medium, then cook for 5 minutes, or until the mixture is reduced and thickened.

Meanwhile, prepare the noodles according to the package directions. Drain the noodles, rinse under cold running water, and drain again. Add the cooked noodles and shrimp to the coconut curry and cook for an additional 2–3 minutes, stirring frequently, until heated through.

Serve immediately, garnished with scallions and sesame seeds.

SERVES 4

2 tbsp vegetable oil

1 small red bell pepper, seeded and diced

7 oz/200 g bok choy, stalks thinly sliced and leaves chopped

2 large garlic cloves, chopped

1 tsp ground turmeric

2 tsp garam masala

1 tsp chili powder (optional)

½ cup hot vegetable stock

2 heaping tbsp smooth peanut butter

1½ cups coconut milk

1 tbsp soy sauce

9 oz/250 g thick rice noodles

10 oz/280 g cooked shelled jumbo shrimp

2 scallions, finely shredded and 1 tbsp sesame seeds, to garnish

WOK-FRIED JUMBO SHRIMP IN SPICY SAUCE

Heat a wok over a medium–high heat, then add the oil. Add the shrimp and stir-fry for about 4 minutes, until they begin to turn pink. Arrange the shrimp on the sides of the wok, out of the oil, then add the ginger and garlic and stir until fragrant. Add the scallion and chili bean sauce. Stir the shrimp into this mixture.

Reduce the heat slightly and add the rice wine, sugar, soy sauce, and stock. Cover and cook for an additional minute. Serve immediately.

SERVES 4

3 tbsp vegetable or peanut oil

1 lb/450 g jumbo shrimp, deveined but unpeeled

2 tsp finely chopped fresh ginger

1 tsp finely chopped garlic

1 tbsp chopped scallion

2 tbsp chili bean sauce

1 tsp Chinese rice wine

1 tsp sugar

½ tsp light soy sauce

1–2 tbsp chicken stock

SHRIMP FU YUNG

SERVES 4–6

1 tbsp vegetable or peanut oil

4 oz/115 g large shrimp, peeled and deveined

4 eggs, lightly beaten

1 tsp salt

pinch of white pepper

2 tbsp snipped Chinese chives

Heat a wok over a medium–high heat, then add the oil. Add the shrimp and stir-fry for about 4 minutes, until they begin to turn pink.

Season the eggs with the salt and pepper and pour over the shrimp. Stir-fry for 1 minute, then add the chives.

Cook for an additional 4 minutes, stirring all the time, until the eggs are cooked through but still soft in texture. Serve immediately.

SHRIMP & PINEAPPLE CURRY

Peel the pineapple and chop the flesh. Heat the coconut cream, pineapple, curry paste, fish sauce, and sugar in a wok until almost boiling.

Shell and devein the shrimp. Add the shrimp and cilantro to the wok and simmer for 3 minutes, or until the shrimp have turned a bright pink color.

Serve the shrimp with steamed jasmine rice.

SERVES 4

½ fresh pineapple

1¾ cups coconut cream

2 tbsp Thai red curry paste

2 tbsp fish sauce

2 tsp sugar

12 oz/350 g jumbo shrimp

2 tbsp chopped cilantro

cooked jasmine rice, to serve

SWEET CHILE SQUID

Place the sesame seeds on a cookie sheet, toast under a hot broiler, and set aside.

Heat a wok over a medium heat, then add 1 tablespoon of the oil. Add the squid and cook for 2 minutes, then remove and set aside.

Add another 1 tablespoon of oil to the wok and fry the bell peppers and shallots for 1 minute. Add the mushrooms and fry for an additional 2 minutes.

Return the squid to the wok and add the sherry, soy sauce, sugar, chile flakes, and garlic, stirring thoroughly. Cook for an additional 2 minutes.

Sprinkle with the toasted sesame seeds, drizzle over the remaining sesame oil, and mix. Serve on a bed of rice.

SERVES 4

1 tbsp sesame seeds

2½ tbsp sesame oil

10 oz/280 g squid, cut into strips

2 red bell peppers, seeded and
   thinly sliced

3 shallots, thinly sliced

1½ cups thinly sliced mushrooms

1 tbsp dry sherry

4 tbsp soy sauce

1 tsp sugar

1 tsp hot chile flakes, or to taste

1 clove of garlic, crushed

cooked plain rice, to serve

JUMBO SHRIMP IN TAMARIND SAUCE

SERVES 2

12 oz/350 g jumbo shrimp, heads removed but unpeeled

1½ tbsp finely chopped fresh ginger

2 shallots, finely chopped

½ green chile, seeded and finely chopped

peanut oil, for frying

3 tbsp chopped fresh cilantro

cooked plain rice, to serve

tamarind sauce

1 tbsp tamarind paste

1 tbsp sugar

2 tsp oyster sauce

2 tbsp water

1 tsp Thai fish sauce

Remove the shells from the shrimp, leaving the last segment and the tail in place. In a small bowl, combine the ginger, shallots, and chile. Combine the sauce ingredients in another bowl.

Heat a wok over a medium–high heat, then add the oil to a depth of ½ inch/1.5 cm. When the oil is almost smoking, add the shrimp and stir-fry for 3–4 minutes, until they begin to turn pink. Remove from the wok and drain in a colander.

Pour off all but 2 tablespoons of oil from the wok, then heat the remaining oil over a high heat. Stir-fry the ginger mixture for 1 minute. Add the tamarind sauce and stir for a few seconds, until hot. Add the shrimp and stir-fry for 1 minute, until the sauce is slightly reduced.

Transfer the shrimp to a warmed serving dish, and garnish with the cilantro. Serve immediately with rice.

VEGETARIAN

HOT & SOUR ZUCCHINI

Put the zucchini slices in a large colander and toss with the salt. Cover with a plate resting on the zucchini and put a weight on top. Let drain for 20 minutes. Rinse off the salt and spread out the slices on paper towels to dry.

Heat a wok over a high heat, then add the peanut oil. Add the Sichuan pepper, chile, garlic, and ginger. Fry for about 20 seconds, until the garlic is just beginning to color.

Add the zucchini slices and toss in the oil. Add the rice vinegar, soy sauce, and sugar and stir-fry for 2 minutes. Add the scallion and stir-fry for 30 seconds. Sprinkle with the sesame oil and seeds and serve immediately.

SERVES 4

2 large zucchini, thinly sliced

1 tsp salt

2 tbsp peanut oil

1 tsp Sichuan pepper, crushed

$\frac{1}{2}$ –1 fresh red chile, seeded and thinly sliced

1 large garlic clove, thinly sliced

$\frac{1}{2}$ tsp finely chopped fresh ginger

1 tbsp rice vinegar

1 tbsp light soy sauce

2 tsp sugar

1 scallion, green part included, thinly sliced

a few drops of sesame oil

1 tsp sesame seeds

EGGPLANT STIR-FRY WITH HOT & SOUR SAUCE

First prepare the sauce. Combine the soy sauce, rice vinegar, and sugar in a small bowl, stirring to dissolve the sugar. Mix in the cornstarch paste and stir until smooth.

Slice the eggplants in half lengthwise. With the flat side facing down, slice each half lengthwise into ½-inch/1-cm strips. Slice the wider strips lengthwise in half again, then cut all the strips crosswise into 1½-inch/4-cm pieces.

Heat a wok over a high heat, then add 5 tablespoons of the oil. Add the eggplant and bell pepper strips and stir-fry for 2–3 minutes, until just beginning to color. Remove from the wok and drain on paper towels.

Heat the remaining tablespoon of oil over a high heat. Stir-fry the water chestnuts, scallions, ginger, garlic, and chile for 1 minute.

Return the eggplant and red bell pepper to the wok. Reduce the heat to medium and add the soy sauce mixture and the hot stock. Stir-fry for 2–3 minutes, until slightly thickened. Garnish with sesame seeds and sliced scallion tops. Serve with rice.

SERVES 4

2 eggplants, peeled

6 tbsp peanut oil

2 red bell peppers, seeded and thinly sliced

8 oz/225 g canned water chestnuts, drained and sliced

6 scallions, sliced

2 tsp finely chopped fresh ginger

1 large garlic clove, thinly sliced

1 fresh green chile, seeded and finely chopped

⅔ cup hot vegetable stock

1 tsp sesame seeds, to garnish

thinly sliced scallion tops, to garnish

cooked plain rice, to serve

sauce

1½ tbsp soy sauce

1½ tbsp rice vinegar

2 tsp sugar

2 tsp cornstarch, blended to a smooth paste with a little water

BROCCOLI WITH PEANUTS

SERVES 4

3 tbsp vegetable oil or peanut oil

1 lemongrass stalk, coarsely
   chopped

2 fresh red chiles, seeded and
   chopped

1-inch/2.5-cm piece fresh ginger,
   grated

3 kaffir lime leaves, coarsely torn

3 tbsp Thai green curry paste

1 onion, chopped

1 red bell pepper, seeded and
   chopped

1 large head broccoli, cut into
   florets

4 oz/115 g green beans

scant ½ cup unsalted peanuts

Put 2 tablespoons of the oil, the lemongrass, chiles, ginger, lime leaves, and curry paste into a food processor or blender and process to a paste.

Heat a wok over a medium heat, then add the remaining oil. Add the spice paste, onion, and bell pepper, and stir-fry for 2–3 minutes, until the vegetables start to soften.

Add the broccoli and green beans, cover, and cook over a low heat, stirring occasionally, for 4–5 minutes, until tender.

Meanwhile, toast or dry-fry the peanuts until lightly browned. Add them to the broccoli mixture and toss together. Serve immediately.

MUSHROOMS & GREEN BEANS WITH LEMON & CILANTRO

Rinse the mushrooms and dry with paper towels. If using clumping mushrooms, such as enoki and buna shimeji, slice off the root and separate the clump. Slice cremini mushrooms in half.

Heat a wok over a medium–high heat, then add the oil. Add the coriander seeds and bay leaf, and fry for a few seconds to flavor the oil. Add the mushrooms and beans and stir-fry for 5 minutes.

Stir in the garlic, lemon juice, and soy sauce. Season with salt and black pepper and stir-fry for 2 minutes. Sprinkle with the cilantro, sesame oil, and sesame seeds and fry for a few seconds. Serve hot, warm, or at room temperature.

SERVES 2

1 lb/450 g mixed small mushrooms, such as cremini, enoki, and buna shimeji

6 tbsp canola oil

1 tsp crushed coriander seeds

1 fresh bay leaf

6 oz/175 g green beans

1 large garlic clove, thinly sliced

3 tbsp lemon juice

2 tsp soy sauce

2 tbsp chopped fresh cilantro

2 tsp sesame oil

2 tsp sesame seeds

salt and pepper

SPICY TOFU WITH RICE

To make the marinade, mix the stock, cornstarch, soy sauce, sugar, and chile flakes together in a large bowl. Add the tofu and toss well to cover in the marinade. Set aside to marinate for 20 minutes.

Heat a wok over a medium–high heat, then add 2 tablespoons of the oil. Stir-fry the tofu with its marinade until brown and crispy. Remove from the wok and set aside.

Heat the remaining oil in the wok and stir-fry the ginger, garlic, and scallions for 30 seconds. Add the broccoli, carrot, bell pepper, and mushrooms and cook for 5–6 minutes. Return the tofu to the wok and stir-fry to heat through. Serve immediately with rice.

SERVES 6

9 oz/250 g firm tofu, rinsed, drained, and cut into ½-inch/ 1-cm cubes

4 tbsp peanut oil

1 tbsp grated fresh ginger

3 garlic cloves, crushed

4 scallions, thinly sliced

1 head broccoli, cut into florets

1 carrot, cut into thin sticks

1 yellow bell pepper, seeded and thinly sliced

2¾ cups thinly sliced shiitake mushrooms

cooked plain rice, to serve

marinade

5 tbsp vegetable stock

2 tsp cornstarch

2 tbsp light soy sauce

1 tbsp superfine sugar

pinch of chile flakes

AGEDASHI TOFU

SERVES 2

²/₃ cup water

2 tsp dashi granules

2 tbsp shoyu (Japanese
   soy sauce)

2 tbsp mirin

vegetable oil, for deep-frying

10½ oz/300 g silken tofu, drained
   on paper towels and cut into
   4 cubes

2 tbsp all-purpose flour

garnish

1 tsp grated fresh ginger

2 tsp grated daikon

¼ tsp kezuri-bushi shavings

Put the water in a pan with the dashi granules and bring to a boil.
Add the shoyu and mirin and cook for 1 minute. Keep warm.

Heat a wok over a high heat. Pour in the oil and heat to
350°F/180°C, or until a cube of bread browns in 30 seconds.
Meanwhile, dust the tofu cubes with the flour.

Add the tofu to the oil, in batches, and cook until lightly golden
in color. Remove, drain on paper towels, and keep hot while you
cook the remaining tofu cubes.

Put 2 pieces of tofu in each of 2 bowls and divide the dashi stock
between them. Garnish with ginger, daikon, and kezuri-bushi.

OYSTER MUSHROOMS & VEGETABLES WITH PEANUT CHILI SAUCE

Heat a wok over a high heat, add the oil, and heat until almost smoking. Stir-fry the scallions for 1 minute. Add the carrot and zucchini and stir-fry for 1 minute, then add the broccoli and cook for an additional minute.

Stir in the mushrooms and cook until they have softened and at least half the liquid they produce has evaporated. Add the peanut butter and stir well. Season with the chili powder to taste. Finally, add the water and cook for an additional minute.

Serve with rice and garnish with lime wedges.

SERVES 6

1 tbsp vegetable or peanut oil

4 scallions, finely sliced

1 carrot, cut into thin sticks

1 zucchini, cut into thin sticks

½ head broccoli, cut into florets

9 cups oyster mushrooms, thinly sliced

2 tbsp crunchy peanut butter

1 tsp chili powder, or to taste

3 tbsp water

cooked plain rice, to serve

lime wedges, to garnish

SWEET & SOUR VEGETABLES ON NOODLE PANCAKES

Prepare the noodles according to the package directions. Drain well and snip into 3-inch/7.5-cm pieces, then set aside.

Meanwhile, prepare the vegetables as necessary and chop into equal-size chunks.

Beat the eggs in a large bowl, then stir in the noodles and scallions and season to taste with salt and pepper. Heat an 8-inch/20-cm skillet over a high heat. Add 1 tablespoon of the oil and swirl it around. Pour in one quarter of the egg mixture and tilt the skillet so it covers the bottom. Reduce the heat to medium and cook for 1 minute, or until the thin pancake is set. Flip it over and continue cooking until the pancake is set. Keep warm in a low oven while you make 3 more pancakes.

When you have made 4 pancakes, heat a wok over a high heat, then add the remaining oil. Add the thickest vegetables, such as carrots, first and stir-fry for 30 seconds. Gradually add the remaining vegetables and the bamboo shoots. Stir in the sauce and stir-fry until all the vegetables are tender and the sauce is hot. Spoon the vegetables and sauce over the pancakes and serve.

SERVES 4

4 oz/115 g fine rice noodles

2 lb/900 g selection of vegetables, such as carrots, baby corn, mushrooms, broccoli, snow peas, and onions

6 eggs

4 scallions, sliced diagonally

2½ tbsp peanut or corn oil

3½ oz/100 g canned bamboo shoots, drained

scant 1 cup store-bought sweet-and-sour sauce

salt and pepper

ASIAN VEGETABLES WITH YELLOW BEAN SAUCE

SERVES 4

1 eggplant

salt

2 tbsp vegetable oil

3 garlic cloves, crushed

4 scallions, chopped

1 small red bell pepper, seeded and
   thinly sliced

4 baby corn, halved lengthwise

scant 1 cup snow peas

7 oz/200 g green bok choy,
   coarsely shredded

14½ oz/425 g canned straw
   mushrooms, drained

4 oz/115 g fresh bean sprouts

2 tbsp Chinese rice wine or dry
   sherry

2 tbsp yellow bean sauce

2 tbsp dark soy sauce

1 tsp chili sauce

1 tsp sugar

½ cup chicken or vegetable stock

1 tsp cornstarch

Cut the eggplant into 2-inch/5-cm long thin sticks. Place in a
colander, then sprinkle with salt and let stand for 30 minutes.
Rinse in cold water and dry with paper towels.

Heat a wok over a medium–high heat, then add the oil. Add
the garlic, scallions, and bell pepper and stir-fry over a high heat
for 1 minute. Stir in the eggplant pieces and stir-fry for an
additional minute, or until softened.

Stir in the baby corn and snow peas and stir-fry for 1 minute.
Add the bok choy, mushrooms, and bean sprouts and stir-fry
for 30 seconds.

Mix the rice wine, yellow bean sauce, soy sauce, chili sauce,
and sugar together in a bowl, then add to the wok with the stock.
Bring to a boil, stirring constantly.

Slowly blend the cornstarch with the water to form a smooth
paste, then stir quickly into the wok and cook for an additional
minute. Serve immediately.

CHINESE VEGETABLES & BEAN SPROUTS WITH NOODLES

Heat a wok over a medium–high heat and bring the stock, garlic, and ginger to a boil. Stir in the noodles, red bell pepper, peas, broccoli, and mushrooms and return to a boil. Reduce the heat, cover, and let simmer for 5–6 minutes, or until the noodles are tender.

Meanwhile, preheat the broiler to medium. Spread the sesame seeds out in a single layer on a cookie sheet and toast under the broiler, turning to brown evenly—watch constantly because they brown quickly. Tip the sesame seeds into a small dish and set aside.

Once the noodles are tender, add the water chestnuts, bamboo shoots, napa cabbage, bean sprouts, and scallions to the wok. Return the stock to a boil, stir to mix the ingredients, and let simmer for an additional 2–3 minutes to heat through thoroughly.

Carefully drain off 1¼ cups of the stock into a small heatproof pitcher and set aside. Drain and discard any remaining stock and turn the noodles and vegetables into a serving dish. Quickly mix the soy sauce with the reserved stock and pour over the noodles and vegetables. Season with pepper and serve at once.

SERVES 4

5 cups vegetable stock

1 garlic clove, crushed

½-inch/1-cm piece fresh ginger, finely chopped

8 oz/225 g medium egg noodles

1 red bell pepper, seeded and sliced

¾ cup frozen peas

½ cup broccoli florets

3 oz/85 g shiitake mushrooms, sliced

2 tbsp sesame seeds

8 oz/225 g canned water chestnuts, drained and halved

8 oz/225 g canned bamboo shoots, drained

10 oz/280 g napa cabbage, sliced

5 oz/140 g fresh bean sprouts

3 scallions, sliced

1 tbsp dark soy sauce

pepper

CRISP NOODLE & VEGETABLE STIR-FRY

Heat a wok over a high heat. Pour in the oil and heat to 350°F/180°C, or until a cube of bread browns in 30 seconds.

Add the noodles, in batches, and cook for 1½–2 minutes, or until crispy and puffed up. Remove and drain on paper towels. Pour off all but 2 tablespoons of oil from the wok.

Heat the remaining oil over high heat. Add the green beans and stir-fry for 2 minutes. Add the carrot and zucchini, mushrooms, and ginger and stir-fry for an additional 2 minutes.

Add the napa cabbage, scallions, and bean sprouts and stir-fry for an additional minute. Add the soy sauce, rice wine, and sugar and cook, stirring constantly, for 1 minute.

Add the chopped cilantro and toss well. Serve immediately, with the noodles.

SERVES 4

peanut or sunflower oil, for deep-frying

4 oz/115 g thin rice noodles, broken into 3-inch/7.5-cm lengths

4 oz/115 g green beans, cut into short lengths

2 carrots, cut into thin sticks

2 zucchini, cut into thin sticks

4 oz/115 g shiitake mushrooms, sliced

1-inch/2.5-cm piece fresh ginger, shredded

½ small head napa cabbage, shredded

4 scallions, shredded

3 oz/85 g fresh bean sprouts

2 tbsp dark soy sauce

2 tbsp Chinese rice wine

large pinch of sugar

2 tbsp coarsely chopped fresh cilantro

SPICY NOODLES WITH MUSHROOM EGG ROLLS

SERVES 4

2 tbsp vegetable or peanut oil

1 small onion, chopped finely

8 oz/225 g mushrooms, chopped

1 tbsp Thai red curry paste

1 tbsp Thai soy sauce

8 square egg roll skins

vegetable or peanut oil,
   for deep-frying

8 oz/225 g egg noodles

1 garlic clove, chopped

6 scallions, chopped

1 red bell pepper, seeded and
   chopped

1 tbsp ground coriander

1 tbsp ground cumin

Heat a wok over a medium–high heat, then add 1 tablespoon of the oil. Stir-fry the onion and mushrooms until crispy and browned. Add the curry paste and soy sauce and stir-fry for 2–3 minutes. Remove the wok from the heat.

Spoon an eighth of the mixture across one of the egg roll skins and roll up, folding the sides over the filling to enclose it.

Clean the wok and heat over a high heat. Pour in the oil and heat to 350°F/180°C, or until a cube of bread browns in 30 seconds. Deep-fry the egg rolls, 4 at a time, until crispy and browned. Drain on paper towels and keep warm.

Meanwhile, prepare the noodles according to package directions.

Heat the remaining oil in the wok and stir-fry the garlic, scallions, and red bell pepper for 2–3 minutes. Stir in the coriander and cumin, then drain the noodles and add them to the wok. Toss together and serve topped with the egg rolls.

MUSHROOM & TOFU LAKSA WITH NOODLES

Puree the spice paste ingredients in a food processor, pulsing several times until smooth.

Heat a wok over a medium-high heat, add the spice paste, and stir-fry for 30 seconds. Pour in the stock and coconut milk and bring to a boil. Add the mushrooms, tofu, and tomato paste and season to taste with salt and black pepper. Simmer gently for 5 minutes.

Meanwhile, cook the noodles according to the package directions. Divide between four large soup bowls. Ladle the spicy broth over the noodles. Serve.

SERVES 4

3½ cups vegetable stock

14 oz/400 g canned coconut milk

9 oz/250 g shiitake mushrooms, stalks removed, thinly sliced

1 cup cubed firm tofu

2 tbsp tomato paste

6 oz/175 g fine egg noodles

salt and pepper

spice paste

2 fresh red chiles, seeded and chopped

1½-inch/4-cm piece fresh ginger, chopped

2 large garlic cloves, chopped

2 lemongrass stalks, tough outer layers discarded, inner stalks chopped

1 tsp coriander seeds, crushed

6 macadamia nuts, chopped

8 cilantro roots with short length of stem attached, or small handful of fresh cilantro

3 tbsp vegetable oil

SICHUAN NOODLES

Peel the carrot and cut off both ends, then grate it lengthwise on the coarsest side of a grater to make long, thin strips. Set the carrot strips aside.

Cook the noodles according to the package instructions. Drain and rinse under cold running water to stop the cooking, then set aside.

Heat a wok over a high heat, then add the oil. Add the garlic and onion and stir-fry for 1 minute. Add the vegetable stock, chili bean sauce, sesame paste, ground Sichuan peppercorns, and soy sauce and bring to a boil, stirring to blend the ingredients together. Add the bok choy quarters and carrot strips and continue stir-frying for 1–2 minutes, until they are just wilted. Add the noodles and continue stir-frying, using 2 forks to mix all the ingredients together. Serve the noodles when they are hot.

SERVES 4

1 large carrot

9 oz/250 g thick egg noodles

2 tbsp peanut or corn oil

2 large garlic cloves, very finely chopped

1 large red onion, cut in half and thinly sliced

½ cup vegetable stock or water

2 tbsp chili bean sauce

2 tbsp Chinese sesame paste

1 tbsp roasted and ground dried Sichuan peppercorns

1 tsp light soy sauce

2 small bok choy or other Chinese cabbage, cut into quarters

BROCCOLI & SNOW PEAS STIR-FRY

SERVES 4

2 tbsp vegetable or peanut oil

dash of sesame oil

1 garlic clove, finely chopped

1½ cups small broccoli florets

1 cup snow peas

3 cups thickly sliced Chinese cabbage

5–6 scallions, finely chopped

½ tsp salt

2 tbsp light soy sauce

1 tbsp Chinese rice wine

1 tsp lightly toasted sesame seeds

Heat a wok over a medium–high heat, then add the oil. Add the garlic and stir-fry vigorously. Add all the vegetables and salt and stir-fry over a high heat, tossing rapidly, for about 3 minutes.

Pour in the soy sauce and rice wine and cook for an additional 2 minutes. Sprinkle with the sesame seeds and serve hot.

VEGETARIAN

297

GARLIC SPINACH STIR-FRY

Heat a wok over a high heat, then add the oil. Add the garlic, black bean sauce, and tomatoes and stir-fry for 1 minute.

Stir in the spinach, chili sauce, and lemon juice and mix well. Cook, stirring frequently, for 3 minutes, or until the spinach is just wilted. Season with salt and pepper. Remove from the heat and serve immediately.

SERVES 4

6 tbsp vegetable oil

6 garlic cloves, crushed

2 tbsp black bean sauce

3 tomatoes, coarsely chopped

2 lb/900 g spinach, tough stalks removed, coarsely chopped

1 tsp chili sauce, or to taste

2 tbsp fresh lemon juice

salt and pepper

SPICY VEGETARIAN STIR-FRY

Heat a wok over a medium–high heat, then add 2 tablespoons of the oil. Add the turmeric and a pinch of salt. Carefully add the potatoes, stirring continuously to coat in the turmeric. Stir-fry for 5 minutes, then remove from the wok and set aside.

Heat the remaining tablespoon of oil and stir-fry the shallots for 1–2 minutes. Mix in the bay leaf, cumin, ginger, and chili powder, then add the tomatoes and stir-fry for 2 minutes.

Add the spinach, mixing well to combine all the flavors. Cover and simmer for 2–3 minutes. Return the potatoes to the wok and add the peas and lemon juice. Cook for 5 minutes, or until the potatoes are tender.

Remove the wok from the heat and discard the bay leaf, then season with salt and pepper. Serve with cooked basmati rice.

SERVES 4

3 tbsp vegetable oil

½ tsp turmeric

8 oz/225 g potatoes, cut into ½ inch/1 cm cubes

3 shallots, finely chopped

1 bay leaf

½ tsp ground cumin

1 tsp finely grated fresh ginger

¼ tsp chili powder

4 tomatoes, coarsely chopped

10½ oz/300 g spinach, trimmed and coarsely chopped

generous 1 cup fresh or frozen peas

1 tbsp lemon juice

cooked basmati rice, to serve

salt and pepper

RED CURRY
WITH MIXED
LEAVES

SERVES 4

2 tbsp peanut oil or vegetable oil

2 onions, thinly sliced

1 bunch of fine asparagus spears

1¾ cups coconut milk

2 tbsp Thai red curry paste

3 fresh kaffir lime leaves

8 oz/225 g baby spinach leaves

2 heads bok choy, chopped

1 small head Chinese cabbage,
  shredded

handful of fresh cilantro, chopped

cooked plain rice, to serve

Heat a wok over a medium–high heat, then add the oil. Add the onions and asparagus and stir-fry for 1–2 minutes.

Add the coconut milk, curry paste, and lime leaves and bring gently to a boil, stirring occasionally. Add the spinach, bok choy, and Chinese cabbage and cook, stirring, for 2–3 minutes, or until wilted. Add the cilantro and stir well. Serve immediately with rice.

VEGETARIAN

303

CARROT & PUMPKIN CURRY

Pour the stock into a large saucepan and bring to a boil. Add
the galangal, half the garlic, the lemongrass, and chiles, and
let simmer for 5 minutes. Add the carrots and pumpkin and let
simmer for 5–6 minutes, until tender.

Meanwhile, heat a wok over a medium–high heat, then add the
oil. Stir-fry the shallots and the remaining garlic for 2–3 minutes.
Add the curry paste and stir-fry for 1–2 minutes.

Stir the shallot mixture into the pan and add the coconut milk
and Thai basil. Let simmer for 2–3 minutes. Serve hot, sprinkled
with the toasted pumpkin seeds.

SERVES 4

²⁄₃ cup vegetable stock

1-inch/2.5-cm piece fresh
   galangal, sliced

2 garlic cloves, chopped

1 lemongrass stalk (white part
   only), finely chopped

2 fresh red chiles, seeded and
   chopped

4 carrots, peeled and cut into
   chunks

8 oz/225 g pumpkin, peeled,
   seeded, and cut into cubes

2 tbsp vegetable oil or peanut oil

2 shallots, finely chopped

3 tbsp Thai yellow curry paste

1³⁄₄ cups coconut milk

4–6 fresh Thai basil sprigs

2 tbsp toasted pumpkin seeds,
   to garnish

CABBAGE & COCONUT CURRY

Puree the spice paste ingredients in a food processor or blender, adding a splash of water to moisten.

Heat a wok over a medium–high heat, then add the oil. Fry the mustard seeds until they start to crackle. Reduce the heat to medium, then add the onion and stir-fry until golden. Stir in the spice paste and stir-fry for 30 seconds.

Add the shredded cabbages and pour in the water, stirring well so the cabbages are covered with the paste. Season with the crushed peppercorns and a little salt. Cover and cook over low heat for 7–10 minutes, stirring occasionally to prevent sticking.

When the cabbages are tender, add the coconut flakes, cilantro, and lime juice. Stir for a minute to heat through and serve.

SERVES 4–6

3 tbsp vegetable oil

1 tsp mustard seeds

1 small onion sliced

¼ white cabbage, core removed, leaves shredded

½ small green cabbage, core removed, leaves shredded

⅓–½ cup water

½ tsp crushed black peppercorns

4 tbsp toasted coconut flakes

3 tbsp chopped cilantro

juice of ½ lime

salt

spice paste

1¾ oz/50 g creamed coconut, melted

1 green chile, seeded and roughly chopped

1 tbsp finely chopped fresh ginger

2 garlic cloves, sliced

1 small onion, finely chopped

½ tsp salt

1 tsp cumin seeds

½ tsp ground turmeric

EGGPLANT & BEAN CURRY

SERVES 4

2 tbsp vegetable or peanut oil

1 onion, chopped

2 garlic cloves, crushed

2 fresh red chiles, seeded and chopped

1 tbsp Thai red curry paste

1 large eggplant, cut into chunks

4 oz/115 g small eggplants

generous 1 cup baby fava beans

4 oz/115 g green beans

1½ cups vegetable stock

2 oz/55 g creamed coconut, chopped

3 tbsp Thai soy sauce

1 tsp jaggery or light brown sugar

3 kaffir lime leaves, coarsely torn

4 tbsp chopped fresh cilantro

Heat a wok over a medium–high heat, then add the oil. Sauté the onion, garlic, and chiles for 1–2 minutes. Stir in the curry paste and cook for 1–2 minutes.

Add the eggplant and cook for 3–4 minutes, until starting to soften. (You may need to add a little more oil because the eggplant will soak it up quickly.) Add all the beans and stir-fry for 2 minutes.

Pour in the stock and add the creamed coconut, soy sauce, sugar, and lime leaves. Bring gently to a boil and cook until the coconut has dissolved. Stir in the cilantro and serve hot.

ZUCCHINI & CASHEW NUT CURRY

Heat a wok over a medium–high heat, then add the oil. Stir-fry the scallions, garlic, and chiles for 1–2 minutes, until softened but not browned.

Add the zucchini and mushrooms and cook for 2–3 minutes, until tender.

Add the bean sprouts, cashew nuts, chives, and soy sauce and stir-fry for 1–2 minutes.

Serve hot with rice or noodles.

SERVES 4

2 tbsp vegetable or peanut oil

6 scallions, chopped

2 garlic cloves, chopped

2 fresh green chiles, seeded and chopped

1 lb/450 g zucchini, cut into thick slices

4 oz/115 g shiitake mushrooms, halved

½ cup fresh bean sprouts

½ cup toasted or dry-fried cashew nuts

few Chinese chives, chopped

4 tbsp Thai soy sauce

cooked plain rice or noodles, to serve

EGG FRIED RICE WITH VEGETABLES & CRISPY ONIONS

Heat a wok over a medium–high heat, then add the oil. Stir-fry the garlic and chiles for 2–3 minutes.

Add the mushrooms, snow peas, and baby corn and stir-fry for 2–3 minutes. Add the soy sauce, sugar, and basil, then stir in the rice.

Push the mixture to one side of the wok and add the eggs to the bottom. Stir until lightly set, then combine with the rice mixture.

Heat a second wok to medium–high, then add the remaining oil. Stir-fry the onions until crispy and brown. Serve the rice topped with the onions.

SERVES 4

4 tbsp vegetable or peanut oil

2 garlic cloves, chopped finely

2 fresh red chiles, seeded and chopped

4 oz/115 g mushrooms, sliced

2 oz/55 g snow peas, halved

2 oz/55 g baby corn, halved

3 tbsp Thai soy sauce

1 tbsp jaggery or light brown sugar

few Thai basil leaves, plus extra to garnish

3 cups cooked and cooled rice

2 eggs, beaten

2 onions, sliced

EGG FU YUNG

SERVES 4–6

2 eggs

½ tsp salt

pinch of white pepper

1 tsp melted butter

2 tbsp vegetable or peanut oil

1 tsp finely chopped garlic

1 small onion, finely sliced

1 green bell pepper, seeded and
   finely sliced

3 cups cooked rice, chilled

1 tbsp light soy sauce

1 tbsp finely chopped scallions

5 oz/150 g fresh bean sprouts

2 drops of sesame oil

Beat the eggs with the salt and pepper. Heat the butter in a skillet and pour in the eggs. Cook as an omelet, until set, then remove from the skillet and cut into slivers.

Heat a wok over a medium–high heat, then add the oil. Stir-fry the garlic until fragrant. Add the onion and stir-fry for 1 minute, then add the bell pepper and stir-fry for an additional 1 minute. Stir in the rice and when the grains are separated, stir in the soy sauce and cook for 1 minute.

Add the scallions and egg strips and stir well, then finally add the bean sprouts and sesame oil. Stir-fry for 1 minute and serve.

INDEX